HOLDING TOGETHER

HOLDING TOGETHER
COURAGE FOR LIFE'S PAIN AND STRUGGLES

Eric A. Forseth

DORDT COLLEGE PRESS

Cover by Rob Haan
Layout by Carla Goslinga
Cover photo Copyright 2016 by Jan Forseth, ImagesOfTheWild.
com

Printed in the United States of America.

Dordt College Press   www.dordt.edu/DCPcatalog
498 Fourth Avenue NE
Sioux Center, Iowa 51250

ISBN: 978-1-940567-17-4

The Library of Congress Cataloging-in-Publication Data is on file with the Library of Congress, Washington, D.C.
Library of Congress Control Number: 2016955284

This book is dedicated to the Forseth and Rozendal family and all the families that are holding together through life's unexpected pain and struggles.

TABLE OF CONTENTS

PREFACE

My mother lived an amazingly full life, even though she struggled with Multiple Sclerosis (M.S.) for twenty-four years. For many years I've considered writing a book about my family's experiences as the nine of us sought to cope with the consequence of her illness. When my wife Kim was recently diagnosed with M.S., I felt even more compelled to write about these experiences. Why am I compelled to share this information with others? There are many reasons to share one's life experiences with others, but the primary reason that I want to "document" some of our family experiences is to share how Scripture has inspired our family to overcome the everyday trials and tribulations of Multiple Sclerosis. Throughout this book, I refer to a specific verse in the Bible and then relate it to a personal experience. That I include specific references to my parents, siblings, spouse, or children is not that important; they merely illustrate that every family goes through trials and tribulations. What is important though is the perspective or the "lens" through which we view these opportunities of life.

A bit of family history will provide a frame of reference. Fred and Jean Forseth (my parents) initially resided in Aberdeen, South Dakota. My father's side of the family had emigrated from Norway to North Dakota. My mother's side of the family had emigrated from Friesland to Iowa. There were seven children in our family. Of the seven children, I was the middle child. When I was three years old, our family moved from South Dakota to Denver, Colorado. The three other children in this move were my older sisters Jan, Carol, and Lora. Shortly after arriving in Denver, one of my younger brothers Ron was born. Two years later, the twins Jay and Sandra were born. This is when the twists in the road developed with my mother's health. Immediately after giving birth to the twins, my mother developed what I have come to characterize as pregnancy-onset Multiple Sclerosis. Within a very short timeframe after my mother came home from the hospital, she transitioned from needing to use a cane, to a walker, to a wheelchair. With two infants, and seven children in all, and a mother who could not walk, our family was desperate.

My father worked in the insurance industry as a property and casualty underwriter. During this time of family crisis, he came up with a plan to help us cope with our family's desperate situation, but one that would also influence culture. With no way of being able to raise seven children and take care of an disabled spouse by himself, he rather spontaneously decided to consider having unwed mothers come into our home to take care of the family needs, all the while helping these mothers forego an abortion and get back into the working world. My father was an expert with insurance details, so this ended up working out well for the unwed mothers. We would advertise in the local papers, "Unwed Mothers Welcome to Apply," and then we would briefly explain our desperate family situation. From then on we had a sequential supply of unwed mothers to help take care of our family. We would in turn provide them a "safe haven" as they waited for the birth of their child. On average, they would live with us for 6–12 months. After their babies were born, the mothers would stay with us for a brief period of time; but often we would help them transition to a new living situation. My father saw this as an opportunity to shape culture. Knowing that society would often condemn these unwed mothers, even though they were in a tough situation, my dad saw this as an opportunity to offer Christ's redemption to a situation where a life could be changed.

Over the course of the twenty-four years that my mother had M.S., our family hosted fifty-five individual "employees" who came in and helped take care of my mom and the seven children. While these young women served in our home, my mother would witness to them about the saving blood of Jesus. She would challenge them to become Christians. She saw the call to disciple and share the Great Commission as a privilege. One woman, the fifteenth of the fifty-five that served in our home, was named Jackie Russell. My mother led Jackie to the Lord during her pregnancy. Ironically, this unwed mother led me and several of my brothers and sisters to accept Jesus Christ as our personal savior. She paused and prayed with us one evening and cited John 3:3: Unless one is born again, you cannot enter the Kingdom of God. How ironic that an individual led to the Lord by our mother would in turn lead us to the Lord. A story of God's providence and faithfulness had just unfolded.

While my mom prioritized the great commission and our responsibility to understand and communicate the doctrine of salvation, my father was anchored in the cultural mandate to subdue the earth. My dad's way to fulfill the calling to subdue the earth was to recognize that we are all sinners, and that any way Christ can redeem a sinner is an opportunity to give God dominion over all areas of life. Dad is a quiet man. He is actually very shy. His calling of co-creating here on earth was to gracefully help individuals like unwed mothers overcome their sinful way of life so that the grace of God could permeate their lives. He really is the unsung hero in the whole family. Fittingly, he never was much for recognition. He was always a fan of quiet contributions versus loud ovations.

This book is about a journey of God's unfolding love. It is about a covenant relationship of parents investing in their children. It is also about making the most of dire circumstances. We lived a simple life that was modeled by both parents. This is also a story of nurture as much as nature. Nurture was a key factor of our mom's investment in our lives. What you will read about isn't normal because we really never achieved a normal life because each day was so different. John Ortberg wrote a book called *Everybody's Normal Till You Get to Know Them*. One insight of his book is that really no one is normal and that we all are accountable to each other. That was true of our family – it was a story of living in community and no one was more important than the other. I would go so far as to say that no one grows up in a "normal" home. Everyone has trials and tribulations and hopefully the illustrations you read about here will inspire you to stay the course and make the most of your individual family situation.

In addition to my childhood experience with M.S., a few years ago my wife was diagnosed with M.S. People have shared with me that I was more likely to win the lottery than to have both my mother and spouse have M.S. It was a devastating phone call to receive when my wife called me one afternoon to share that an initial neurology appointment had revealed the likely diagnosis of M.S. This book is also about dealing with devastating news. Living life to the fullest regardless of circumstances is a calling we have as we serve in God's Kingdom. I hope you can get a glimpse of God's Kingdom while reading this book.

This book is an autobiography of my experiences. My brothers and sisters might well have a different perspective on some of the events I recount. For example, later on in her life, one physician changed my mother's diagnosis from M.S. to Amyotrophic Lateral Sclerosis (A.L.S., also known as Lou Gehrig's Disease). Personally, I never gave much credence to this diagnosis because there was always a desire to know more about whatever disease mom had and the diagnosis was less important to me than our family's coping with the day-to-day challenges. I mention this because I'm sure several of my brothers and sisters would claim citing A.L.S. in this book is just as important as citing M.S. as the malady that took the wind out of my mom's physical sails. I'm more persuaded than ever that, by the time mom died at age 55, she had lived an amazingly full life, regardless of whether she had M.S. or A.L.S. She lived a full life by the way she shared Christ's love with others in spite of her circumstances. The journey was extraordinary because of her positive attitude and amazing disposition. I hope you can see a glimpse of this in the pages that follow.

Let me introduce you to the seven Forseth siblings.

- Jan, the oldest daughter, is a nature photographer who travels the world.

- Carol, born a year after Jan, serves as a contractor accountant and bid specifications manager.

- Lora, two years younger, is a registered nurse and is recently recovering from breast cancer.

- Eric serves in college administration at a Christian college in Iowa.

- Ron presently serves as vice-president of Outreach and general manager of sermoncentral.com.

- Jay, one of the twins, previously served as a college vice-president and now serves as a pastor.

- Sandra, the other twin, served twenty-five years as a teacher for the U.S. Center for World Mission.

Enjoy the contents of this book. Journey with me on the battle with M.S. See God's hand shape a family and seven children in miraculous ways. Grow deeper in God's Word. Challenge yourself to be discipled and to disciple others. Thank you for allowing me to share a glimpse of his kingdom. I'll count it a privilege if these words help your life to be transformed by Scripture, God's grace, and his divine hand in the years ahead.

PERPLEXED BUT NOT IN DESPAIR

My father is somewhat of a practical joker. It was a coping mechanism that was fairly helpful most of the time. The last two children born in the family were twins. The oldest of the twins by a few minutes was a boy. The second twin was a female that was born ten minutes after the doctor had already left the room. The nurse actually thought it was the contents of the afterbirth. Can you imagine carrying twins for nine months and not even realizing twins were going to be the end product of the day? Mom was just starting to show signs of M.S. shortly before the twins were born. The trauma of the childbirth of two left her weak and in the hospital longer than expected.

Shortly after the twins were born, dad, trying to deal with two opposite gender children, started out on this journey of twins with a coping mechanism. The first call made to announce the births was to Grandma Rozendal. Grandma picked up the phone in Aberdeen, South Dakota. "Good news. We had a little BOY. Mom is doing okay but she is extremely tired. Can't talk much now, but we wanted to share the news about a little BOY being born." The next call was to Grandma Forseth, also in Aberdeen, South Dakota. "Good news. We had a little GIRL. Mom is doing okay but she is extremely tired. Can't talk much now, but we wanted to share the news about a little GIRL being born."

Next, Grandma Rozendal called Grandma Forseth to discuss the new grandbaby. The conversation went like this. "Did you hear the news about a new baby boy," said Grandma Rozendal. "A baby boy?" said Grandma Forseth. "That isn't what Fred told me. I heard it was a baby girl." They were perplexed. They decided to have one grandparent call the hospital back and get the straight scoop. Shortly after they hung up, Grandma Rozendal called back to the Denver hospital and asked for the Jean Rozendal Forseth hospital room. My dad (Fred Forseth) picked up the phone. "Fred, you told me you had a boy. Grandma Forseth said you told her that you had a girl. Which one is it, Fred?" Dad promptly replied, "It is both!" You can imagine how frustrated Grandma Rozendal was, but she took it in stride and promptly got off the phone and called across town to the other grandma and shared the full information on the twins.

It is so easy in life to become downcast, as this Scripture verse indicates. Dad's coping mechanism of humor and jesting really was more than a coping mechanism. Dad didn't let circumstances in life get him down. Can you imagine going into a hospital room, your wife having unexpected twins, and a short time later finding out your wife also has M.S.? It would have been so easy to fall into despair. Instead, dad put his hope in God and his praise was clearly evident in the smiling way he let the grandmas know that the blessing of twins had just rounded out the number of children to a total of seven.

It is so easy to become perplexed and live in despair. We have all met individuals with this type of disposition. When circumstances seem overwhelming, stop the pathway of despair and live in a spirit of gratitude and praise. And sure, a bit of humor can also help with overcoming life's struggles.

Prayer: Lord, thank you for opportunities to praise you in all areas of our life. Forgive us Lord when we allow ourselves to become downcast. Help us Lord to see the bright side of life and to live in praise rather than in despair. Bring friends and family into our lives that help season our disposition with praise and encouragement. Thank you for the opportunity to acknowledge you daily as our Savior and God. Amen.

The LORD has heard my cry for mercy; the LORD accepts my prayer.
Psalm 6:9

BEING ACCEPTED

In growing up, my mother often spoke of acceptance. Her focus on acceptance was different than others. She was a prayerful individual. Day in and day out, she prayed fervently. Many times her prayers were on behalf of others. The exciting aspect of her prayers involved a focus on countercultural thoughts and deeds. You see, we were a taboo family. Taboo in that people often stared at my mother because she was in a wheelchair. She couldn't walk because of her Multiple Sclerosis. Even at a young age, I had the taboo task of taking my mother to the bathroom. Not the greatest pleasure of a young boy under the age of ten. But we were also a taboo family because we impacted culture and walked alongside sinners because we were sinners ourselves. When I was six, we decided to try and re-direct culture by influencing unwed mothers with a depth of love for them so that they could regain esteem and get back into the working world.

We would advertise in the newspaper, "unwed mothers welcome to apply to help our family." We were desperate. We were crying for mercy to somehow take care of seven children, a mother with Multiple Sclerosis, and her two youngest children needing to be raised as twin infants. God answered our prayer when we cried out. A mother with Multiple Sclerosis cried out for healing, not for herself or her maladies, but for healing of past sins that resulted in unexpected pregnancies. Unwed mothers were encouraged to avoid an abortion and engage the sanctity of life. The countercultural effort included bringing the unwed mothers with our family when we were out in public. Not only did my mother get strange stares because of her disability, but the unwed mothers turned even more heads than a person in a wheelchair. Acceptance by others wasn't a high priority because what we were doing to discourage abortions was taboo.

I've often thought of how we seek acceptance from others. We seek acceptance into cliques of friends. We seek acceptance into churches. We seek acceptance into colleges. We even seek acceptance into the strangest circles, including positions of power, positions of influence, and positions of importance. Who or what are you trying to be accepted by? How can you shift your focus of acceptance from man's acceptance to God's acceptance? This verse clearly calls us to cry out for mercy. And in turn the Lord will accept us. Who do you need to cry out for? The downtrodden need mercy too. Have you ever thought about crying out for those that are not part of accepted circles? Who else do you know that needs mercy? Because we have all sinned and fallen short of the glory of God, we should acknowledge the daily need for mercy. Ask God for mercy to look inside ourselves and identify shortcomings and not project these pitfalls on others. Consider crying out for mercy to see others as being created in God's image so we can live more redemptively. Mercy, grace, and truth are evident when other's stares do not make you feel unaccepted. A focus on God's acceptance is a rarity that is first accessible when we cry out for mercy.

Prayer: Lord, help us to cry out for mercy. Help us to acknowledge that this mercy isn't about man's acceptance. Help us to see this mercy is to give us eyes to see our own shortcomings and that staring at others isn't the best means for projecting our weaknesses. Give us your acceptance God, which is best found in supporting others who need redemption as much as we do. Thank you for allowing us to give you dominion over all areas of our thoughts, deeds, words, and actions. Amen.

> Barnabus . . . sold a field he owned and brought the money and put it at the apostles' feet. Acts 4:37

ENCOURAGEMENT IN SPITE OF HARDSHIP

Have you ever wondered what it would be like to truly be so grace-filled and encouraged that "there are no needy persons amongst yourselves." I can honestly say amidst a family of seven children, and a mother that could not walk or care for any of her children's physical needs, few of our needs went unmet. How could this be so? Truth be said, we had a mom (and a dad) that essentially sold themselves out and brought all their resources to their children's and spouse's feet.

I'm sure you know Barnabas means "encouragement." How was it possible for a person like Barnabas to sell his field and put this money at the apostle's feet? My gut says there was selfless leadership going on with this group of believers and that no one was keeping score. Our childhood experiences saw the same selfless leadership. Picture this: Early in the morning, a father would quickly get dressed and then he had the insurmountable task every day of dressing his spouse, taking her to the bathroom, and then placing her in a hospital bed in the living room. After this routine, one of the seven children fed mom. Then it was off to the races. Mom was selflessly giving herself away in spite of hardship. Giving herself away included the following type of actions. She would encourage each child as they prepared to go to school. Comments shared included "I love you, I believe in you, and I know you will do well." No pity party about being an invalid. No feeling sorry about hardships. No fretting about spending the next eight hours in a hospital bed waiting for the children to come home.

I've often wondered how we can be so self-absorbed when we really aren't going through that many hardships compared to others. Do you wonder if you can give yourself away in the same way Barnabas did? Could the following types of actions allow you to give yourself away? Listening instead of responding. Giving instead of receiving. Sharing instead of asking. Serving instead of being served. Learning to do with less instead of always wanting more.

Encouraging others instead of discouraging them.

My mother encouraged us every day. Every day she gave herself away. She could have sobbed and sobbed for years but she chose the higher ground. She encouraged me by challenging me to work hard. She encouraged me by challenging me to be humble. She encouraged me by challenging me to serve others. She encouraged me by helping me reach my full potential. She built up each child's self-esteem with words. The reason why there weren't many needs around our house is because we learned that we were whole beings. Mom demonstrated encouragement to us because she said that as whole beings our spiritual, emotional, social, intellectual, and physical needs were all tied together. Each day, she said it was our responsibility to give every bit of ourselves to God and others. She daily challenged us to take the focus off ourselves and seek to meet the needs of others. It was true encouragement because if anybody had a reason to feel sorry for oneself, and be discouraged, it was her. Have you come to the end of your rope? Are you discouraged? Take some time today and look around. Acknowledge how fortunate you are and find a way to take your resources and put them at other people's feet. You do have a choice. God has dominion over your ability to encourage as much as he has dominion over your physical resources or farmland. Ask him to help you give yourself away today.

Prayer: Lord, forgive me for focusing on my petty needs. Challenge me to be a source of encouragement to others. Take my eyes off physical needs and guide me in helping to see colleagues and family members as whole individuals that need my encouragement today. Amen.

And Jesus grew in wisdom and stature, and in favor with God and man.
Luke 2:52

STANDING TALL

My mom was a person of stature. She was a very tall woman: approximately 5'11" from what I remember. This height came from the Rozendal Dutch heritage. But she had stature in many other forms. She had spiritual depth, she had doctrinal foundations, and she lived transformationally despite her circumstances. And somehow she modeled an appropriate balance between these three strands.

In regards to spiritual depth, she lived in a way that was Christocentric. In providing a twenty-four-year panoramic view of her usual week day, she would start with breakfast and help her children get out the door for school. The help she provided the children was focused on bolstering the confidences of the children to brave the day. After the kids departed, mom would focus on developing her stature through prayer. This would entail one to two hours of quiet time. Then, she would often listen to Scripture with audio recordings. After this, she would usually pause for lunch and a short siesta. After lunch and a respite, she would listen to books on tape. Usually, these books were theologically focused and they often challenged her to deepen her doctrinal foundations. The remainder of her day was spent building others up.

The living out of Scripture in all she did was by far the most amazing aspect of her life. This transformational lifestyle included the following types of efforts and manifestations. These gestures included a smile no matter what, influencing unwed mothers in our home by coping with a degrading disease with such a positive attitude, and challenging whoever she came in periodic contact with to consider being selfless.

Have you ever thought about how your physical gestures influence others? Being willing to smile is a matter of stature that is underestimated. A smile is the most powerful nonverbal way of communicating. But how often do we underestimate this nonverbal cue? Here is a woman who was incapacitated as an invalid in a wheelchair for twenty-four years but she somehow overlooked her own circumstances to give a smile away to others.

Another unique aspect of mom's day was a willingness to encourage unwed mothers towards positive alternatives. She was "tall in stature" in this form by, plain and simple, just encouraging unwed mothers with the redemption of Jesus Christ. Even though sin transpired (as it does in all of us), mom would encourage unwed mothers with the redeeming value of acknowledging that sin can be covered by blood of Jesus.

Last but not least, mom modeled the stature of a selfless attitude. She could have complained each and every day. I don't recall her complaining about her physical situation. The only time she really registered a concern was when she had a bladder infection and the pain became unbearable. She modeled selflessness in her day by listening to others. She was an amazing listener. She asked leading questions to each of the children as they entered the house from mid-afternoon until late in the evening. Perhaps she lived a simple life, but you also can be a person of stature and wisdom by growing in spiritual depth, in doctrinal understandings, and in living out a life that models and encourages transformation.

Prayer: Lord, help us to better understand what it means to be a person of stature. Help us to better know when to pause for prayer and Scripture. Give us a desire and a heart to grow our intellect in doctrinal understandings. Call us to live a transformational life by serving others selflessly. Amen.

Come, let us bow down in worship, let us kneel before the LORD our Maker; for he is our God and we are the people of his pasture, the flock under his care. Psalm 95:6–7

WORSHIP – WHAT DO YOU BOW DOWN TO

My mother considered all of her thoughts, deeds, actions, and attitudes as a form of worship. Whether it involved guiding her children for twenty-four years from a wheelchair, meeting with a neighbor friend to study Scripture, or giving her undivided attention to one of the unwed mothers, she worshipped God in every aspect of her life. I've often thought but never shared with anyone out loud, "if you really heard yourself complain, you would embarrass yourself because you really don't have much to complain about." Why would I think this versus sharing this out loud?

Frankly, we all have idols in our lives. It is a daily temptation to separate this or that from being under God's dominion. In my mother's situation, she could have kept "idols" such as:

- An evening walk with their spouse around the block
- Waterskiing around a resort lake
- Fishing in a mountain stream
- Shopping at the local mall
- Attending a concert
- Working 8–12 hours a day
- Planting a garden
- Going out for coffee with a good friend

Not that these are wrong, but my mom just couldn't do anything remotely like the above because of her physical disability. I've often thought her life was richer because she lived so simply. She didn't bow down to very much on this earth because she didn't have access to very much. Somehow she did live Christianly in her daily life choices. She worshipped by considering others to be more important than herself. She gave her undivided attention away every day. Although she couldn't kneel, she would bow often in her heart to pray for others. She saw herself as a caretaker of others.

Now that my wife has been diagnosed with Multiple Sclerosis too, I've been reflecting on what I worship. Through this second lifetime experience of a family member being stricken with this disease, I've re-evaluated my priorities. I've become more cautious about kneeling down to seek praise from others, looking for happiness through "things," or believing that joy is found in earthly pleasures.

A friend of mine has recently written a few books on achieving one's full potential in service (worship) to God. Included in these suggestions are reading more and developing new friendships so you can be challenged to develop into your full potential. Many distractions in life prevent us from feeding our minds and guarding our hearts. As you evaluate your tendencies of worship, what would you be willing to give over to God because he is sovereign?

Prayer: God, forgive us when we have a blurry focus and displaced priorities. It is so easy in your kingdom to think that some items are okay to worship and some items aren't worth worshipping. In reality, everything we do is a form of worship. Call us to honor you in all we do. Amen.

So do not be ashamed of the testimony about our Lord or of me his prisoner. Rather, join with me in suffering for the gospel, by the power of God. He has saved us and called us to a holy life – not because of anything we have done but because of his own purpose and grace. 2 Timothy 1:8–9

JOIN WITH ME IN SUFFERING

I was recently reading my brother's account of my mother's attitude towards suffering. Because of her quick progress towards becoming wheelchair-bound in less than a year, she suffered side effects from inactivity. Whether it was a painful bladder infection or muscle spasms that were out of control, there was plenty of visible and physical suffering. However, I've often wondered about the nonphysical suffering. Mental anguish, jealousy, coveting a healthy lifestyle, desires for mobility, and plain and simple depression can be components of suffering. My brother shared, "there were times though, that she did get in a pouty mood and would mope, refuse to be comforted, or at least try and elicit some sympathy." I imagine this was because with her usual great attitude, the family members probably "lost the sense" of just how hard it was for her to be incapacitated.

What does it mean to join someone in their suffering? The context of the above verses is helpful in understanding this question. 2 Timothy 1:7 mentions that "the Spirit God gave us does not make us timid, but gives us power, love and self-discipline." To join someone in their suffering is a call to compassion and a call to boldness. I can vividly remember that most individuals stared at my mother because of her disability. Most individuals were also fearful to help. Probably not because they didn't know how to help, they just possessed timidity (likely due to unfamiliarity with disabilities at that time).

Aspects of the preceding verse point to a component of self-discipline before the context is given by Paul to "join with me in suffering for the gospel." In reality, self-discipline is what one needs to join someone in their suffering. Self-discipline could take on the characteristics of "getting out of your comfort zone" and reaching out to help someone in less fortunate circumstances. What does it mean to exercise self-discipline in these situations? Time, prayer, and compassion are components of this discipline.

Time is the most precious component of self-discipline. We all have the opportunity (not obligation) to stop what we are doing and help someone in need. We might open a door, mow a neighbor's lawn, or help a person with disabilities with regular day-to-day needs like going to the bathroom. Prayer for a person in need is another opportunity to join someone in their suffering. Praying for healing, for attitudes or circumstances to improve, and for learning to cope is another way to join with someone in their suffering. For some, compassion and empathy could be the most meaningful way in which to join someone in suffering. Are you willing today to stop what you are doing, listen to someone in need, and join them for a conversation that includes empathizing with their situation? By far the most meaningful efforts in joining my mom (or my wife) in their suffering have included when friends stop by unannounced. Usually these friends are functioning under God's grace and purposes and not under their own obligations or self-imposed holiness.

Do you need to stop what you are doing today and go join someone in their suffering?

Prayer: Lord, help us to be sensitive to our neighbors, family members, and friends. Somehow, give us the power to focus on others instead of on ourselves. Also Lord, when it comes to conveniences or desires for more amenities, help us somehow to keep a perspective that allows us to suffer for the Gospel with purpose and grace. Teach us to seek your power to make a difference for you. Amen.

Not only so, but we also glory in our sufferings, because we know that suffering produces perseverance; perseverance, character; and character, hope. Romans 5:3–4

JOY THROUGH PERSEVERANCE

My mother often talked about the importance of joy. She didn't equate it with happiness. She equated it with a frame of mind. She would say, "Son, you really don't fully understand real suffering until you have been through what I've been through. But, my afflictions are only temporary and every day I have an opportunity to be joyful." And somehow she lived this out each and every day. Her face gleamed with joy. She was a model of perseverance. She lived with joy regardless of her circumstances, but this didn't mean she was always happy. It meant she was willing to trust God and bring him glory through her sufferings.

How is this so? How do we bring God glory through our sufferings? The Scripture verse here indicates a sequence of experiences. First, we know that suffering produces perseverance, perseverance develops character, and character develops hope. I've often wondered how some people have more hope than others. I think the answer to how one accesses hope is simple, but acting upon the answer is what is difficult.

Real life illustrations of suffering included basic life needs in our family. You see, when a person is an invalid and they become immobile, basic faculties of eating and voiding must be tended to or physical suffering will result. Periodically, my mom would need to go to the bathroom, and because of the family's crazy schedules, she would be unable to void in a timely manner. Every so often this would lead to a bladder infection that caused her unintended pain and suffering. Regardless, mom would have a glow on her face that indicated she was asking God to help her remain stable through this suffering. This was a measure of character. She had this deep character that allowed her to face any circumstance in God's timing. This character evolved into an everyday hope for her. She lived out this everyday hope by radiating the importance of giving God the glory in all we say and do. It would have been easy to curse

God. It would have been easy to give up hope. But, she never did because of the depth of perseverance, character, and hope that was cultivated in her life. Regardless of circumstances, she constantly focused on others rather than on herself.

How about you? What suffering have you been through lately? Perhaps your suffering has included more than physical suffering. Have you been mischaracterized? Are you going through a low time or a form of depression? Is some of your suffering just due to a lack of clarity regarding the future? Through all of this, God clearly calls us to the next levels of perseverance, character, and hope. This is where we find joy – which is often not the same thing as happiness. The depth of knowing God better is our true joy – a depth that is possible when we allow God to mature us through suffering to perseverance, character, and hope.

Reach out to others today and encourage them with your God-given joy. In God's everyday blessings joy is possible in whatever circumstance you face.

Prayer: God, we have been called by you to live a joyful life. There are times when it is easy to feel sorry for ourselves and get stuck in a myriad of circumstances. Help us Lord to move past the stage of suffering and into the depths of character development and hope. Through all that we encounter, somehow Lord, call us to a joy that only you can provide. We ask that you encourage us with a "centeredness" of hope and allow us to see our sufferings as temporary. Thank you Lord for bringing us to a depth of love that allows us to see through our circumstances, give you the glory, and live out your joy. Amen.

But he said to me, "My grace is sufficient for you, for my power is made perfect in weakness." Therefore I will boast all the more gladly about my weaknesses, so that Christ's power may rest on me. 2 Corinthians 12:9

FINDING JOY IN WEAKNESSES

The above Scripture was my mother's favorite verse. She often quoted it, and I really never understood why until reflecting upon this in the past few years. Why would anyone want to focus on their weaknesses? I don't yet have a full answer to this, but I'm compelled to believe that we are called to give everything to God, including our weaknesses.

Here are some of the weaknesses my mom had. She couldn't walk. She had an obsession for details. While my dad was an introvert, she was an extrovert. She was a truly social being. However, because of the devastating effects of M.S., towards the end we had to read her lips when she tried to speak. This was hard on her because she craved social interaction. She couldn't sing anymore either and this was hard for her. She had previously cut a record and so few people knew about this. Why share these types of intimate details? My mom often shared with us about her weaknesses to cultivate humility in her children. She would say, "You may be overemphasizing something here on earth when God intended it for good; we are called to give him our shortcomings too."

Mom was saying in her own words, don't lose perspective. Perspective for her was acknowledging that with God's grace, we can access God's power to overcome our earthly weaknesses. But "earthly weaknesses" can mean something different for each of us. For some, physical challenges may be the focus of their weaknesses. For others, emotional, mental, or social challenges will mark their weakness. The bottom line is that we are all "bankrupt" in some way with weaknesses, but how we live within our weaknesses is the key factor of this Scripture. My mom lived within her weaknesses by being transparent. She would say "I find joy in my weaknesses." But then she would say more importantly, "God is using these weaknesses in a powerful way." How? Mom saw in each of her children innate, God-given talents that needed to be cultivated.

She overcame her weaknesses by selflessly focusing on others with encouragement. Humans have a tough time extending grace. Mom would somehow be a truth-teller, but she would always end what she had to say with words of encouragement and grace. That is how Christ's power rested on her. It should rest on us in a similar fashion.

Another way mom overcame weaknesses was her willingness to boast singularly in God's perfect power. Her sense of humor consistently allowed others to laugh with her about weaknesses. She didn't mock her weaknesses but somehow she humbly made fun of them. There is a lesson here. Don't take yourself too seriously. Find a way to "boast all the more gladly" about how God created you. What weaknesses do you need to work through today? Have you allowed circumstances, people, or things to overwhelm you? God's promise is that we can overcome our weaknesses by humbly acknowledging them and that his power can "perfectly" work through these opportunities. How should you reach out to others today and focus less on your weaknesses and in turn focus on how God is calling you to use your strengths? If God has called you to encourage, then encourage. If God has called you to mentor, then mentor. If God has called you to minister to others, then minister. If God has called you to teach, then teach. We overcome our weaknesses by being willing to ask God to help us move towards our strengths.

Prayer: Lord, help us to surround ourselves with friends that complement our weaknesses. Also, encourage us to push aside the devil's efforts to over-focus on our human shortcomings. Call us to a purity of service in all we say and do. Help us to boast in your power and perfection. Amen.

So we fix our eyes not on what is seen, but on what is unseen, since what is seen is temporary, but what is unseen is eternal. 2 Corinthians 4:18

PERSPECTIVE – THE GLASSES WE WEAR

Have you ever met someone who clearly has an eternal perspective? After you talk with such an individual, you come away enriched because they have challenged you to have a kingdom perspective. Somehow with all her afflictions, my mom was able to challenge others to improve their perspective. Conversations went like this. "Do you understand how you have been given so much? Do you understand there is always going to be someone in a better situation than you and in a worse situation that you? Do you realize how you are losing perspective because of your focus?"

Frequently, life can get blurry. With our different lenses on life, we can easily lose perspective. When criticized, discouragement can easily prevail. When praised, rose-colored-glasses fit so well. As we grow older, we develop a lens that tells us this isn't fair. When someone disparages our name or reputation, we develop a critical spirit lens.

One of my favorite mentors taught me to choose my lens on living everyday with care. He would often say, "Don't pay too much attention to criticism and also don't overpay attention to praise." In his own special way, he was encouraging a longer, eternal view of life. It is so easy to obsess about what is right in front of us. These challenges may include bills that need to be paid, the next week of work that looks unbelievably impossible, a marriage relationship that is starting to fracture, or a health situation that is less than promising. But God calls us to focus on what is unseen. Stated another way, he asks us to remain faithful.

I have often wrestled with describing what "being faithful" means. My mom explained it this way. She said faithfulness is an attitude – a willing attitude in which we are able to trust God with our future one day at a time. Have you ever met people who think they can control each and every situation? It just isn't possible. God calls us to fix our eyes on what we cannot see. This includes trusting him wholeheartedly with our finances, family, work, friendships, marriages, and everything else. If he is the Lord of our life, he is Lord of everything.

Have you ever asked yourself, what is toughest for me to trust God with? Do you trust him with your problems, with the future, with your past, and with your next few hours? I can hear my mom's voice through this dilemma; one we face each day. She would remind me that "The earth is the LORD's and everything in it, the world, and all who live in it" (Psalm 24:1). We need to realize that what is unseen allows us hope for the future. How we trust God with this hope for the future is the essence of life. Trusting God is the lens through which we are called to view life.

How we focus our lens on life is the most important decision we make each day. Are you focused on how you can help other people or are you only focused on your own immediate problems? Are you focused on serving others or are you focused on others serving you? Challenge yourself today to have your "eye doctor" (and your "mind doctor") assess the appropriateness and adequacy of your current lens on life. Focusing on what is seen can be a dangerous way to live. This verse is saying that focusing on gratifying the immediate is not how we are supposed to live. We are supposed to focus on what is unseen and to imagine God's kingdom being perfected. Are you using your imagination today to advance his kingdom?

Prayer: Lord, help me to improve my sight by focusing on the eternal. Please sharpen my vision. In the interim, help us be an agent of redemption in what you entrusted to us. Amen.

"You did not choose me, but I chose you and appointed you so that you might go and bear fruit – fruit that will last – and so that whatever you ask in my name the Father will give you." John 15:16

WHAT IT MEANS TO BE CHOSEN

This verse was without a doubt been the most discussed verse at our house during the growing up years. Mom could explain it so well to each of her children. She would constantly remind us of the responsibility to bear fruit. She would graciously say, "Because God has chosen you, you have a calling to serve others." I've often reflected on mom's centered approach to bearing fruit and how this has guided her seven children in finding their callings.

Here is how this approach has challenged each of us in our professional pursuits. Jan is now an international photographer, travelling the world to take photographs of God's creation. Carol is an accounts manager of a large firm in Colorado, using her expertise to manage financial matters for others. Lora is a nurse. Her caring and compassion is clearly evident even though she recently went through a tough battle with breast cancer. Eric – that's me – has served in Christian education for over thirty years. Ron is vice-president of a para-church organization that helps churches impact their neighborhoods and the general manager of the largest sermon repository in the world. Jay is a pastor, after serving as vice-president of a college. Sandra worked at the U.S. Center for World Mission for 25 years. As you can see, bearing fruit was the guiding theme of mom's influence.

To be chosen to serve in God's kingdom brings a sense of responsibility to fulfill the nobility of this calling. Regardless of the profession we are called to serve in, we have a responsibility to participate in bringing redemption to his kingdom. How are you called to bring redemption in your life? Are you searching for ways to live a more meaningful life? Clearly God is calling us all to bear fruit with what we have been given. Because he has chosen us, we are called to make a difference for others. Have you considered how you are utilizing your God-given talents and whether you should refocus your energies to bear different fruit than the normal?

In regards to being chosen and bearing fruit, today's Scripture verse also states that whatever we ask in Jesus' name, the Father will give us. I don't think he is saying that we can ask for anything in the world and God will give it to us *carte blanche*. We are supposed to read his words in their context and the context here is that we are chosen. Because we are called to bear fruit, when we pray specifically about the fruit God has called us to bear, we can ask God to help us at any time. Avoid being selfish in asking God to help expand the impact of your professional calling. Regardless of your line of work or your future line of work, seek God's face each day on how you can bear fruit.

Now I'm wondering if you fully understand what asking for this calling symbolizes. I'd encourage you to reflect upon what bearing fruit means to you personally. I'd encourage you also to reflect upon what it means to be chosen and how you can acknowledge this in your daily service. Most importantly, I'd encourage you to contemplate carefully which "cup" you ask for in regards to professional callings. If you are going to serve effectively in his kingdom, you will want to seek God's clear guidance on which calling will allow you to use your God-given talents the best. Because we are called to bear fruit that lasts, it is exciting to ponder which next steps we should be taking to serve nobly. Are you ready to move forward in this exciting venture of noble service?

Prayer: God, thank you for choosing us. Thank you for allowing us to bear fruit in your name. Thank you also for your willingness to answer prayer in the context you guide us each day. Amen.

> Jesus commanded Peter, "Put your sword away! Shall I not drink the cup the Father has given me?" John 18:11

ACCEPTING YOUR CIRCUMSTANCES –
A DIFFERENT WAY OF LIVING

Accepting one's circumstances is a different way of living. The different way of living is learning how to make the most of one's circumstances. In dealing with a devastating disease like Multiple Sclerosis, mom was always accepting of her circumstances. She did not let circumstances dampen her happiness.

Have you ever met someone that is short-sighted? Perhaps this person is always complaining about their situation. They carry a "sword" of a bad attitude. They are unwilling to acknowledge God's control in their life and they combat anything and everything that gets in their way. Instead of choosing contentment, they see the glass half-empty and combat their circumstances with a negative attitude. Asking for the cup to be given to someone else is their daily disposition.

I'm grateful that both of my parents were wonderful role models. They never once asked for their circumstances to be altered. They raised seven children in dire circumstances. My mother was unable to walk and hold her infant twins. The preschoolers needed hourly guidance and care. Older siblings needed mentoring and care for nurturing into young adulthood. It would have been easy to abdicate all responsibilities and throw in the towel and say: "Lord, take this cup from me." But neither parent insisted on a change of circumstances. Neither parent pulled a sword and tried to magically cut away a swath of challenges.

How the world thinks and acts can be different from how we think and act as covenant Christians. Did you know the divorce rate for couples with M.S. is now over 75 percent? The world told my parents to consider the easy way out with a divorce. The world is telling me to consider this too. The world says we should seek instant gratification. The world encourages us to focus on self. But that is asking for a cup to be removed instead of dealing with the cup we have been given.

A different cup to drink is a willingness to accept one's circumstances and selflessly focus on someone else's circumstances and needs. My mother was a master of this cup. She constantly found a way to think of others' needs. She prayed for others in their need. She looked outward instead of inward. This willingness to engage the mind and heart and call the hands to service is one of the best cups we can drink.

Consider the cup you have today. Are you consistently focused on your circumstances or are you willing to focus on other people's circumstances? Do you have a desire to help and serve others or do you have a desire to wallow in your day-to-day thoughts? Are you willing to reach outside your circumstances and care deeply for someone in need? When Jesus was given the cup of sacrifice, he had two clear choices. He could pick up the sword and fight against God's will. He chose the second, much tougher choice, to accept his circumstances and become the redeemer of humankind. I'm grateful he set this example for us.

Prayer: Lord, help us to better understand the cup you have given us. Guide us in an attitude that allows us to put down swords and encourages us to carry the cup you have given to us. Help us to reach deeper into your cup so that we can have the strength to understand and embrace the central calling of helping others in their circumstances. Thank you for calling us to a different way of living. Amen.

Some of those present were saying indignantly to one another, "Why this waste of perfume? It could have been sold for more than a year's wages and the money given to the poor." And they rebuked her harshly. "Leave her alone," said Jesus. "Why are you bothering her? She has done a beautiful thing to me. Mark 14:4-6

ALONE BUT NOT PURPOSELESS

Have you ever felt alone? I mean really alone. In this story, a woman broke a jar of perfume and spread the fragrance over Jesus' head to prepare him for what was coming. A group of Pharisees, majoring in minors, questioned Jesus. They insisted money was more important than relationships. Jesus redirected them by indicating later in the chapter that they could give money to the poor after he was gone, but "you will not always have me." Jesus then prodded the locals to change their focus: Why not consider doing beautiful things for others?

Shortly after my mom was stricken with M.S., our family made a bold decision to invest in marginalized people in society that were "alone." We took on the care of unwed mothers. These soon-to-be mothers were alone. At that time, even in the United States, it was taboo to associate with them. They were sinners and people were offended by these women because they made a mistake. One major drawback of being pregnant is that it is so evident. The results of sin sometimes aren't as evident as in these instances, but aren't we all sinners in one form or another?

My mom broke "perfume bottles" over the unwed mothers we housed. She would share with them that we all make mistakes. She would acknowledge past sin in her life. She would shower them with the perfume of kindness by affirming their human value. She rebuked others for the judging of one action and challenged us all to recognize the importance of relationships.

I've often wondered what this woman did for a living before she spread the perfume on Jesus' head. It is apparent Jesus wanted others to leave her alone, but what did she do before performing this "beautiful" action? I suspect she summoned the courage to do this by being in solitude. In the same way, don't we all need to be alone periodically to reflect upon our purposes in life?

As you journey through your day, stop periodically, be alone and check your priorities. Ask yourself if you are spreading perfume or condemnation. I'll never forget how my mother mentored the unwed mothers in our home. Each day she would invest in their human worth. Her perfume was patience. She would help them through rough times and in their daily needs. This willingness to invest in relationship was an outgrowth of my mother's time alone with God. Through prayer, Scripture, meditation, and seeing the world in a different light, my mom was able to sprinkle grace on others' shortcomings.

Today, what do each of us need to do alone to re-focus our purposes? Who do we need to approach with perfume to help them get out of the quagmire of sin? Contemplate what you can do in kindness and compassion.

Prayer: Lord, give me the courage to be alone to allow you to take every portion of my life for building your kingdom. After you have helped me acknowledge my own sin, help me to reach out to others by not looking at their sin but by looking at their potential as someone created in your image. Amen.

Rejoice with those who rejoice; mourn with those who mourn. Romans 12:15

DISCERNMENT FROM THOSE WE TRUST

True friendship involves the active art of empathy. Walking a mile in someone else's shoes requires getting out of one's comfort zone. My mother displayed more empathy than anyone I've met. This skillset included crying with those who were crying, laughing with those who were laughing, praying with those who were praying, celebrating with those who were celebrating . . . and pretty much identifying with whoever was at her side.

But the best tool she had in her empathy skillset was the skill of listening. Do you have a friend that listens with an uncanny ear? To be able to listen is a gift that allows you to rejoice with those who are prepared to rejoice and mourn with those who need to mourn. This listening skill is the foundation of discernment. A friend that has discernment is a friend that you want to partner with for a lifetime.

How do you find a friend that has discernment? I'm not sure you "find" a friend like this. Instead, you become a friend like this. You become a friend like this by being trusted with information, by being confidential, by being willing to listen without judgment. It is a gift to be a discerning friend and if you have two or three of these types of friends in a lifetime, you have been very fortunate.

Another aspect of mom's empathy skills included trust. She would ask leading questions. She would look us in the eyes and inspire our trust. When you talked with her, you would finish the conversation knowing that it ended in confidentiality. The only time I ever remember hearing a second-hand account of what I shared was when dad needed to get involved in a discipline matter. Understandably, there was no confidentiality when it involved a breach of conduct.

Are you building trust with your friendships? Are you asking questions with a listening ear? A discerning friend is discriminant. Although "discriminant" is also a math term, it has an even stronger meaning in how you live. You can be discriminant in all your life choices by basing them on Scripture. When you keep confidence, you are being discriminant. When you are empathetic you are displaying a discriminant attitude. Jesus encourages us to base our day-to-day decisions on discriminant actions and attitudes. This does include weeping with those who weep and rejoicing with those who rejoice, but it means so much more. This Scripture verse is an illustration of how Jesus wants us to live. He is calling us to this paradox by saying yes to rejoicing and weeping but also to everything in between because he is Lord of all aspects of our life.

As you contemplate your day today, strive to be a discerning friend. Listen well. Be empathetic in your actions and attitudes. Be a person of confidence. Consider ways in which you can establish trust.

Prayer: Lord, call us to live the way Christ did. Help us be discriminant. Guide us in all areas of our life, including the highs and lows of life and everything in between. Reveal how we can empathize with others and invest in their rejoicing and mourning. Thank you for allowing us to reach out to others and for shaping us with the discernment only you can provide. Amen.

> "For who is greater, the one who is at the table or the one who serves? Is it not the one who is at the table? But I am among you as one who serves. You are those who have stood by me in my trials." Luke 22:27–28

SERVING WITH LESS NOTORIETY

Jesus is talking to his disciples here at the Last Supper, but in a larger context he is challenging all of us with the rhetorical question: How do you want your epitaph to read? Do you want to be remembered as the person that sat at the table in the banquet room or do you want to be remembered for helping others through their trials? By serving others you may well help them through their trials. I will never forget the friends and family that stood by my mom and dad when they were dealing with challenges related to my mom's M.S. Now, I am faced with similar challenges in connection with my wife's M.S. How are we to conduct ourselves through trials? Let's apply Jesus' words of "I am among you as one who serves."

How do we serve others in the trials of their lives? First of all, serving includes focusing less on yourself and more on others. How do we focus less on ourselves? Rather than just focusing on our own circumstances, we open our eyes to the daily opportunities that surround us to serve others. This may include what we do for others, how we speak to others, or how we listen to others. Take a moment today and step outside your circumstances and selflessly focus on others.

The second thought of serving others is how you focus your mind. Have you ever met someone that is so self-absorbed that they cannot distance themselves from their own circumstances? The Scripture here tells us that one way to move forward is to consider serving. My mom's words of wisdom here were consistently to "get over herself" and recognize that there was always someone who had it much worse than she did. She often would break down in tears by saying, "My body is failing, but I'm so grateful that I still have 100 percent of my mind." She would use her mind to serve others. She challenged people to make the most of their circumstances and move past introspection to developing their God-given strengths.

The third way of serving others is the most important. It has to do with humility. Jesus is talking in this Scripture verse to the disciples about their question of who among them was the greatest. He is basically cautioning them about overemphasizing being at the banquet table. Translated in today's culture, what does this mean to you? Is it important to you who you eat with? Or are you concerned about what house you live in? Are you overemphasizing being first in something? Has something so important to you become an idol? Are you able to enjoy serving as much as receiving attention or recognition?

Overall, Jesus instructs us to stand in community by serving others. Serve with a focus outside of yourself by selflessly thinking of others that are in tougher circumstances than yourself. Step out of your circumstances. Secondly, find a way to occupy your mind differently and find somewhere else you can use your available strengths. Invest in others selflessly by moving past your circumstances. Lastly, worry less about impressions, and more about substance. Find a way to deflect attention from yourself and give God the glory.

Prayer: God, forgive us for focusing on being first at the banquet table. Give us a way through our personal trials by investing in others. Thank you for our circumstances. Speak to us about how we can shift our mind, our introspections, and our concern for accolades. Redeem us today. Amen.

FEARING THE (UN)KNOWN

There have been many books written about how to overcome fears and how to be fearless with hope. I'm going to challenge us to go deeper in dealing with our fears today. Most individuals struggle with the fear of the unknown. This is understandable, but I claim that coping with the fear of the known is just as troublesome.

In the growing up years of my youth, our family struggled with fears of not knowing how M.S. (or A.L.S. according to some diagnoses) would affect our mom's long-term health. Our family had never journeyed through a battle with an autoimmune disease like M.S. We didn't know what to expect. We were afraid of coping with the unknown of a blood clot occurring, dealing with a bad infection that invaded her body due to poor circulation, or responding to a grotesque fall and the next debilitating effects of the disease that would gradually decrease mobility. We sought the Lord often and he answered our prayers by delivering us from our fears. The answers were provided by learning to live one day at a time and coping with those items we could control.

When I fast forward the clock to my present life, I am coping with a fear of the known. We received some really challenging, unfortunate news this week. My wife's M.S. doctor informed her that she is in a relapse and that she has a thoracic plaque developing on her spinal cord. What does this mean in layman's terms? Unless the "hot spot" can be controlled soon, lower leg functionality will likely decrease drastically. Frankly, her mobility has already decreased in the past six months. Now, because of past experiences, I feel the fear of the known. Do I tell my spouse that I feel fear? I don't think so. What are we called to do in light of Scripture? We are called to seek the Lord and anticipate that he will answer our prayers and deliver us from our fears. Thankfully, this includes deliverance even from fears of the known.

How about you? Do you have fears of the unknown or the known? Do these fears include a health situation that doesn't look very promising? How about fears of the known that have to do with dealing with financial troubles, family troubles, or emotional challenges? Some have said that fears of the unknown are the most troubling. I don't think so because some say that 95 percent of our fears of the unknown never come true. Fears of the known are the toughest to deal with because this is the real day to day walk we find ourselves experiencing.

What are we called to do in these situations where hope is potentially limited? The Scripture calls us, even in these situations to seek the Lord, anticipate an answer and delivery from these fears too. My mom was insistent on emphasizing the importance of living one day at a time. She was a model Christian when it came to coping with hardships and fears of the known. I learned from her to be grateful that God's promises include delivery from fears of the known. We serve a mighty God that walks with us daily.

Prayer: Lord, forgive us for not turning to you during times when fears overwhelm us. Help us to cope with fears of the unknown and the known. Guide us Lord in our prayer life and thought processes so we know intimately how you will deliver us from anticipated, real-life challenges. Help us to somehow rest in your promises and give us an inner peace that only you can provide in these circumstances. Thank you for being willing to walk with each of us in this journey of life that includes shortcomings, disabilities, and celebrations. We are grateful that your purposes are fulfilled in redeeming all the areas of our life. Amen.

FEAR GOD, WALK HUMBLY, AND REST IN GIVING GOD THE GLORY

Fearing God is referenced many times in God's Word, but I've often wondered if there is a clear definition for what it means to fear God. Fearing God is often linked to humility. You have likely heard someone say, "This person is a God-fearing man or woman." But what does this mean? In some ways, the fear of God can be seen in how a person carries him or herself, in the way they conduct their lives, in that they walk, talk, and live in a Godly manner. Each time I've heard this shared about someone, there seems to be one common denominator. The person being referred to is usually a person of humility. The link between being humble and fearing God isn't a coincidence.

Is humility learned or is it an acquired trait? I would speculate that humility is primarily a learned trait. Both my mom and my dad were/are God-fearing people. I also think they had to learn unbelievable portions of humility. For instance, early in their marriage, my mom was stricken with what is characterized as pregnancy onset Multiple Sclerosis. Shortly after giving birth to twins, she became severely disabled and was confined to a wheelchair for the remaining portion of her life. The lessons of humility through these experiences were many. They included having someone of the opposite gender needing to take you to the bathroom because it was either that or hold your faculties so long that you suffered other consequences. Other lessons of humility included having someone else feed you, bathe you, and exercise your limbs. The ultimate experience in humility was having a "babysitter" regardless of your age because without a babysitter, and due to the complications of M.S., she ran the risk of choking and asphyxia.

On the flip side, my dad also had to learn active lessons of humility. This included taking his spouse out in public with all eyes on this man pushing a wheelchair. Dad also had the unenviable responsibility of finding a public restroom for women to take his spouse to the bathroom that was meant for the opposite gender. Other lessons included taking care of his spouse's needs each time before his needs could be considered. The list could go on, but you hopefully see the picture.

Through all of these lessons, the fear of God was the primary building block. Because dad had decided to give every portion of his life here on earth for God's glory, he determined first that his family was going to be God-fearing. Snow, rain, or shine, we set off for church every Sunday. To get seven children and an incapacitated spouse "ready to roll" was no easy task. Still, we made our trek each and every week to church, catechism, Sunday school, and more. The lessons continued through the week because both parents lived a God-fearing simple lifestyle.

The fear of God is primary, and the second portion of this Scripture is honor. People that live in humility acquire honor because they deflect honor by living daily for God's glory. Honor comes in different forms when you live Christianly. Seeking honor or paying too much attention to praise and too much attention to criticism is dangerous. Paying attention to how God wants us to live in humility is how he really wants us to live each day.

Prayer: God, help us to see that the way to honor is through humility. Point us in the direction of deflecting praise and seeking to honor you. Humble us in the areas of life that are not glorifying to you. Give us a presence of heart and mind to be re-directed wherever necessary. Thank you for transforming us. Amen.

> I declare to you, brothers and sisters, that flesh and blood cannot inherit the kingdom of God, nor does the perishable inherit the imperishable. Listen, I tell you a mystery: We will not all sleep, but we will all be changed – in a flash, in the twinkling of an eye, at the last trumpet. The trumpet will sound, the dead will be raised imperishable, and we will be changed. 1 Corinthians 15:50–52

VICTORY IN DEATH AND DYING

This Scripture was my mother's second favorite verse. She didn't focus on perishables. She focused on the imperishable (those things of eternal value). I'd like to take you back to when I was sitting in a hospital room with my mother. She was 55 years old. She was dying of pneumonia – actually, it wasn't as much due to pneumonia but due to complications of M.S. She had been in the hospital two weeks and I had spent the night with her to comfort and to read Scripture with her. She had a peace about herself when she died. Her heartrate sped up right around 7 a.m. and then shortly thereafter her heartrate flat lined. I was the only one in the room when she passed. It was a strange feeling.

This experience for me was a defining moment in my life. Although my mom lived only to be 55 years old – she will inherit the kingdom of God because she didn't focus on flesh and blood. She lived on the promise that in a twinkling of an eye, our bodies will be changed. We have the promise of being changed into an imperishable being. This promise is centered in Christ's second coming where those that have been born again (John 3:3, unless you are born again, you cannot inherit the kingdom of God) will awaken from their sleep and be raised imperishable. Being changed is an exciting promise.

Mom lived each day on the promise of being changed. But, she didn't take her adoption in Christ for granted. She dwelt on the kingdom of God and on her responsibility to co-create while here on earth. She gave God the dominion over all her life, including her dire circumstances. Somehow, she dwelt on God's promises about our being raised imperishable and the upcoming consummation when Christ returns.

You may ask, how do we live with the imperishable in mind? How is it that, day after day, a person who spends every day in a wheelchair wakes up with eternal optimism? How did a person who could not take care of one fundamental need become the encouragement and guiding light for seven children? There truly is only one answer. The answer is hidden in this Scripture verse. Flesh and blood cannot inherit the kingdom of God. Translated to modern-day terms, over-focusing on materials of the flesh – physical, mental, social, emotional, or any other earthly happening – is perishable. There for sure is a life-lesson in this for all of us.

How about you? Have you checked yourself today to see where your priorities are placed? I'm not saying that today is when you are going to have victory in death, but I am challenging us all to consider a longer term approach to the decisions we all make in life. Are your decisions based on perishable items? Are you willing to reconsider priorities in your life and to move towards the imperishable?

When mom passed, there was a deep peace about her in spite of her inability for the past twenty-four years to experience the normal "perishables" that most humans are afforded. She didn't have the luxury of deciding which clothes to buy, which car to drive, which house to live in, or how to spend time on the normal perishables. She only had the luxury of seeing others as being created in God's image and, in turn, of investing in the imperishables of their lives.

Prayer: Lord, rid our life of perishables. Thank you changing us with this victory. Amen.

And this is love: that we walk in obedience to his commands. As you have heard from the beginning, his command is that you walk in love. 2 John 1:6

OBEDIENCE. . . ONE STEP AT A TIME

Have you ever met someone that is out of step? Usually this person is out of step because they have a balance issue – a balance issue usually related to a relationship, circumstance, or perspective. I've often wondered if a lack of balance is related to a lack of love and forgiveness. I don't know how for sure, but I'm confident that we as fallen creatures lose our balance when we have lacked love and withheld forgiveness.

As mentors, my parents were forgiving people. Time and again, while being transitioned from her wheelchair to an automobile, mom would accidentally be dropped by one of the children lifting her in or out of the car. It was embarrassing because someone was usually watching. However, mom was forgiving and she dealt with it via her keen sense of humor. She would laugh. She would cry. She was always willing to immediately forgive. I've thought about how this generous portion of forgiveness helped her to keep such a perspective in and through the rigors of daily routines.

Mom (and dad) were able to offer generous portions of forgiveness because they were obedient people. One parent would put on love by not harboring bitterness and generously offering forgiveness. The other would put on love by reaching out to others in need. It was all centered in love. Their first step was to love others – one of the central commands of the Gospel.

How about you? Are you walking in obedience? Or have you been overwhelmed by the daily rigors of life and held onto bitterness rather than giving a generous portion of forgiveness. It is so easy to be out of step in life. There are so many distractions. We all experience distractions in our relationships and interactions have been tarnished because of the sin in our life. Distractions in how we look at things can also draw us to disobedience. We have a natural tendency to create all sorts of idols in our lives, and in loving these we fail to love who and as we ought. Even the circumstances of life can cause us to rationalize our falling short in loving our neighbor.

How can we become more obedient? I believe the answer is to take one step at a time. Every morning, we had the arduous responsibility of helping mom walk one step at a time. We would put on her leg braces, prop her up, and essentially try and get her to lift her legs one step at a time. It wasn't much fun to help with this. But it was an amazing life lesson. We are called to live this way – take one step at a time in love and forgiveness.

Walking one step at a time has different meanings for each of us. For some, it may mean stopping by a family member's house and asking for forgiveness. For others, it may mean removing idols that have developed in our lives and seeking God's forgiveness. And then for others, it may simply entail focusing less on personal circumstances and taking a step of love by helping out in your local community or church projects. There are many ways we can love others. Consider asking yourself – how can I walk in obedience and give portions of love that are inspired by God's commands?

Prayer: Lord, help me to take the first step today and walk in obedience. Show me how to love more deeply and to forgive more generously. Also, somehow call me to action and obedience by removing blinders occasioned by relationships, circumstances, and perspective. Help me to love in tandem with your commands. Amen.

When Jesus' followers saw what was going to happen, they said, "Lord, should we strike with our swords?" And one of them struck the servant of the high priest, cutting off his right ear. But Jesus answered, "No more of this!" And he touched the man's ear and healed him. Luke 22:49–51

THE MIRACLE OF PHYSICAL TOUCH

Have you ever thought about the miracle of physical touch or about the difference that not being able to touch or be touched by someone you love would make in your life? One of my siblings has noted having missed more of our mother's physical touch during childhood. Because of our mother's battle with Multiple Sclerosis, she was not able to embrace her children. The younger children especially missed her physical touch during their early childhood years.

Jesus' touch is mentioned many times in the Bible. Often, when people touched him, they were instantly healed. This Scripture verse tells us of when Jesus reached out and touched a servant's bleeding ear with his healing hand. Too often today touch is deemed inappropriate. This Scripture illustrates the power of human touch and how it really can make a positive impact on others.

The privilege of touch is limited in today's society because of connotations that are associated with inappropriate touching. This is truly saddening. We as humans need to experience the power of physical touch. Physical touch can be affirming in that it can be healing, it can be directional and it can be caring. Certain physical touches are appropriate and they are perhaps underutilized today.

The healing properties of physical touch are illustrated in this Scripture verse so well. Jesus reached out and touched the servant's ear and healed him. This touch was a miracle that Jesus initiated to right a wrong done by one of the disciples. Jesus objected when someone struck the high priest's servant's ear and so he reached out and did another miracle when he didn't need to heal in this instance.

All of us have experienced the miracle of physical touch when the touch has been directional. Illustrations of the directional touch in our childhood included individuals such as teachers and family mentors who 'pushed' us as children to become our best. Without this physical touch of pushing us forward, we would have fallen short. Without this touch, we also would have been in a situation where our directional focus would have been lacking. This touch by others provides encouragement that nudges us to learn more in class, accomplish more in co-curricular activities, and at times, to learn more about the power of physical touch when one is unable to receive this type of touch at home.

There is also the caring aspect of physical touch. When a child falls, the physical touch of a mother is invaluable. When we fall into sin and our shortcomings are recognized, the caring touch of our Heavenly Father is also invaluable. This caring touch redirects us to acknowledge our shortcomings and humbly ask God to help pick us up and move forward in his strength. Have you thought lately about the importance of physical touch and appropriately sharing encouragement with others?

Prayer: Lord, thank you for the power of physical touch. Call us to appropriately encourage a child, a colleague, family, and friends with healing, directional, and caring touches. Help us, Lord, to think about the power of human touch in various professions where you have called us to be a unique source of encouragement. For those serving in health, teaching, and the helping professions, please guide us in how to best encourage others. Thank you Lord for the way you provide this healing touch. Amen.

An elder must be blameless, faithful to his wife, a man whose children believe and are not open to the charge of being wild and disobedient. Since an overseer manages God's household, he must be blameless – not overbearing, not quick-tempered, not given to drunkenness, not violent, not pursuing dishonest gain. Rather, he must be hospitable, one who loves what is good, and who is self-controlled, upright, holy and disciplined. Titus 1:6–8

DISTRACTIONS, DISTRACTIONS, DISTRACTIONS

This Scripture verse identifies a few distractions in life, including unfaithfulness, disbelief, disobedience, being blameful and overbearing, hot-temperedness, drunkenness, violence, and dishonesty. The charge is to replace these distractions with hospitality, to love what is good, be self-controlled, honest, holy, and disciplined. Pretty easy and simple? Not really given all the distractions of life that we face each day.

We have so many distractions in daily life. In watching my mother and spouse cope with Multiple Sclerosis, I've seen two individuals cherish a simpler lifestyle as they dealt with a crippling and chronic disease. This discipline has helped them overcome the distractions of life. I've also observed that this leaning towards a simplified life has progressed at the same rate as their disease's symptoms. Can we learn from this that distractions in life are so easy to let in when our daily routines involve very few challenges to overcome? I'd like to try and re-state this from a different perspective. Our focus can become so blurry when we strive to be entertained, seek the thrill of the temporary, demonstrate dishonor by living outside God's commands, insist on our own way, boil over quickly, abuse substances, progress from anger to intent to physically harming others, or fail to keep our promised word. A Godly vision becomes clearer when have a hospitable spirit, which means we practice hospitality in all we do. In this hospitality, we learn to love what is good with God's eyes. In being self-controlled, we can practice honesty, which leads to integrity and holiness. And in this verse, there is a reason why discipline is mentioned last: because discipline can be at its best when the distractions of life are minimized.

This Scripture verse reminds me of the thoughts in 1 Corinthians 13 – initially we see in a mirror dimly, but as we become more Christ like, we see in the mirror more clearly (how best to conduct our lives). Eventually we have a responsibility to be 'set apart' in our actions and attitudes in the way we live each day. We are to conduct our lives within boundaries. Because it is so easy to press against these boundaries and fall into sin, our actions, and then our attitudes fall short. It becomes a vicious circle.

How do we learn to be more self-controlled, honest, and holy when we are blessed with physical health? I'm not sure it is possible to do this without a consistent, prayerful request to ask God to purify our thoughts, words, deeds, and actions. Each and every day, we should consider asking him to help us serve others with hospitality. We should ask him to help us love more deeply. A pursuit of self-control can then transpire by attempting to minimize the distractions of life. After this, we should ask God to inspect us and guide us to be thoroughly honest in all our dealings. Sanctification is a process that allows others to guide us in accountability. All of this is a cycle of discipline that is God-inspired. Are you able to reflect these traits to become more Christ-like in the days ahead?

Prayer: God, lead me in a holy life that is characterized by a clear reflection of Jesus Christ. Help me to learn to avoid distractions in my life. Simplify my life. Simplify my family's life so we can truly live each day serving others. Through all of this, guide us in self-control and ways of honesty. Truly, this is only possible because you have promised to speak into our lives. Thanks for being willing to do this. Amen.

> The precepts of the LORD are right, giving joy to the heart. The commands of the LORD are radiant, giving light to the eyes. Psalm 19:8

RADIANT EYES ARE WORTH A THOUSAND WORDS

The color of my mom's eyes was steel blue. They reminded me of historians' descriptions of Abraham Lincoln's eyes as "steel blue." My mom's bright blue eyes had an expressive radiance. She exuded joy through her eyes. In spite of all her maladies, mom displayed a joy throughout her difficult experiences. My sense was that this joy was centered in her living within the commands of the Lord and that this in turn gave a radiance to her eyes. How can someone speak so loudly through their eyes? We read people's eyes every day. When someone is tired, we can see it in their eyes. When someone is joyful, we can see it in their eyes. When a person is in pain, you can see it in their visual acuity. Day in and day out, we humans speak with a language of the eyes.

The Scripture verse here calls us clearly to recognize that the commands of the Lord are radiant and this gives light to the eyes. As less mature believers, we see how to act in a Christ-like manner "in a mirror dimly." As we become more Christ-like, we see in a mirror more clearly how to become more Christ-like. In other words, the Scripture (God's commands) does readily give radiance and light to see through our eyes how we are to conduct ourselves. How about you? Are others able to see radiance in your eyes? Is this radiance due to an acknowledgement of God's commands speaking into your life? What precepts do you base your daily decisions upon? God does call us to use his Word as a standard for all we say and do. This is much easier said than done. My mother's ability to use verbal affirmations for instruction was clearly rooted in God's precepts and Scripture. This instruction was God-breathed and it reminded all of us of the foundational text found in Hebrews 4:12: "For the word of God is alive and active. Sharper than any double-edged sword, it penetrates even to dividing soul and spirit, joints and marrow; it judges the thoughts and attitudes of the heart." The Word of God exuded from mom's spirit and sometimes it was sharp as a sword and penetrated all the way to our hearts.

Somewhere here we need to make the jump from giving joy from the heart all the way to radiance and light from our eyes. This is a simple connection for some and much more difficult for others. When we have a willingness to live in faith and trust God to guide us day-by-day with his precepts, the Holy Spirit builds a spiritual foundation within us. In turn, this radiance of God's precepts is further shown in the way we see the world and respond to the world. When our heart is burdened with sin that interrupts our lives, the connection to live radiantly and allow our eyes to illustrate a positive light is very limited. As human beings, our heart is our "wellspring of life" and this in turn determines our spiritual welfare.

When our hearts are right and centered in honoring God through his precepts, anything in front of us, big or small, can be covered by his commands. How do we consciously strive to have our hearts be centered in God's precepts? The most important way to accomplish this is to feed the mind with strong doses of Scripture, which helps us all to guard our heart as the wellspring of life.

Prayer: God, give us humility to seek out scriptural guidance each day to bring on your radiance. Amen.

BEING FAITHFUL

This psalm verse frames faithfulness in a unique way. The Scripture begins by pointing out that God's kingdom is an everlasting kingdom. Essentially this calls attention to the fact that Jesus will return again and God's kingdom here on earth will be made perfect again. After this, the Scripture acknowledges that his dominion will endure through all generations. The passage calls us to acknowledge and accept his rule through all generations.

The Scripture verse then transitions to the emphatic statement that the Lord is trustworthy in all he promises. This tells us he will deliver on his proclamations in the Bible. The claim in God's Word is that he is, plain and simple, faithful in all he does. Those are big words to live up to in this ever-changing world and in the daily family challenges that we face. My mom had Multiple Sclerosis. My wife now has Multiple Sclerosis. I've been reflecting deeply on what it means to be faithful through these trying times: trying times five years ago when my wife received the devastating news of her M.S. diagnosis. Even more trying times this week when my wife received word that her thoracic spinal nerves are swelling because she started a different treatment regimen. Stated simply, her nerve sheath is tearing down, and she is having severe difficulty walking. Her left side, especially her leg, is not functioning very well. Her balance is worse than ever.

I've been asking what it means to stay faithful through both of these family situations with my mom and now my wife. There really is only one answer. Taking life one day at a time is a must. This includes doing all I can to support my wife and family. Sometimes I feel a bit like Job. Some friends have said, "Why don't you just give in and get your spouse a wheelchair?" Another individual said, "Just consider having your wife stay at home and don't bring her with you to social events." Most recently, someone chimed in with, "Your wife sure looks tired." I'm sure the person didn't mean for this to be taken in the wrong way. Sometimes, I wonder if friends are saying to me indirectly, "Why don't you just curse God?"

Our family has seen this opportunity to deal with M.S. as a promise versus a curse. Physical health is so often tenuous here on earth. As we deal with the challenges of a chronic disease, we are called back to Matthew 6:34 where it states, "Therefore do not worry about tomorrow, for tomorrow will worry about itself. Each day has enough trouble of its own." This is another one of God's promises that we stand upon each day. We trust God today because he is faithful in all he does. One step at a time and one treatment at a time, we believe in God's dominion and rule in his kingdom.

How about you? Don't we all have situations where circumstances are just overwhelming? Fears become bigger. We end up too far down a road of false imagination. Situations are blown out of proportion. The most comforting thoughts shared by friends have little to do with words. The biggest help is when someone shares small gestures of faithfulness. Thankfully, that happens with good friends.

Prayer: Lord, call us to remain faithful. One step at a time, encourage us to make a difference by reaching out to others with our deeds as much as our words. Thank you for your dominion. Amen.

> The simple believe anything, but the prudent give thought to their steps.
> Proverbs 14:15

THE COMPLEXITIES IN LIFE

Today I was reflecting upon the complexity of life. I'm not really sure why these thoughts came to mind but the sanctity of life was a topic of discussion and I just couldn't get this off my mind. I was reflecting upon the unwed mothers we had in our home over the years. They each had one extremely complicated decision to make. For these young women, it was not simple to decide to honor the sanctity of life. As a family, we would do our absolute best in conversation to encourage them to consider adoption instead of abortion. Frankly, it was a pretty serious topic of discussion for the younger children in our family to be party to. Most of the mothers were between 20 and 25 years old. Most of them did give their babies up for adoption. Some kept their babies and several of those situations worked out extremely well too.

These situations with the unwed mothers contemplating life decisions spurred reflections on the complexity of life. The verse above – "The simple believe anything, but the prudent give thought to their steps" – acknowledges the intricacies of life decisions. When we believe certain decisions can be made without much thought, this Scripture cautions us not to believe just anything. When we embark into a process of thorough investigation before making a decision, the Scripture applauds this as demonstrating prudency. I'm also persuaded that this Scripture suggests that complex life decisions should be made in community.

How about you? Are you going through situations and decisions related to marriage, a new job, a potential relocation, health situations, death of a loved one, retirement, a new business, house loan, family trials, emotional challenges, social issues, change of schools, or anything else that requires the contemplation of a very important decision? Are you facing these very important situations or decisions in the days, weeks, or months ahead? Don't believe just anything anybody says when you are in these complex situations. Ask trusted friends to come alongside you and help you give thoughts to your steps. Just as our family came alongside un-wed mothers and really, really encouraged them to contemplate life-changing decisions, be sure to prudently take your time when considering the future.

Decision-making is far too oversimplified in today's society. In most movies, the plot line is easily resolved within two hours. Sure, most movies are make-believe and I'm not against the movie theater. But, in real life, most decisions are more complex than they are portrayed in a movie. Take time to prudently weigh your options and try not to simplify life-changing decisions. Find a way to consider pros and cons. Pray individually and with your friends. Consider thoroughly how scriptural insights guide you in any potential path. Lastly, enjoy the steps of being prudent and be confident that your decision has been well-thought-out for any next steps.

Prayer: Lord, please forgive us when we simplify life on our own terms. Guide us in how we should read your Word and in how this informs any of our future considerations. Help us to be prudent by also seeking the counsel of others. When we fall short and simplify important decisions, somehow re-direct us to a better path that brings glory to your name. Thank you for tempering our thoughts and actions. Amen.

THE IMPORTANCE OF TEAMWORK

Teamwork isn't specifically mentioned in the Bible, but the word "team" is used in Isaiah to describe how a team of horses pulled a chariot after an unidentified man drove the horses to the city square to make an announcement regarding Babylon. The first words from his mouth after arrival included the pronouncement that Babylon had fallen and that all the images of its gods (small g) lay shattered on the ground.

Teamwork is the initial focus of this Scripture. Have you contemplated what it takes for a team of horses to pull a chariot or a plow? To do this, it takes a unifying effort. The horses' strides need to be in sync with the neighboring horse. The horses' hooves need to land at the same time. The weight balance needs to move forward at the same pace. Without balance, the ride can be bouncy for the chariot driver.

Noting this emphasis on unified teamwork helped me reflect on the importance of how our family chose to work as a team. Three older sisters really became surrogate mothers to the younger children by raising them from very young ages. Teamwork was especially important for the twin babies that were born to a mother who couldn't even hold her own children. Teamwork in our family also included cooking, doing the dishes, cleaning the house, and doing chores. Then, the biggest challenge of all included knowing one's role in a family of seven children. Emotionally, it was important to encourage those that were doing well and challenge younger siblings that needed to carry more weight. Spiritually, we challenged each other to brave the storm. Physically, we needed teamwork to fulfill basic needs including taking mom to the bathroom and changing the diapers of younger kids. Socially, we had to give each other space to allow for a sense of humor and balance.

Are you involved with a team or are you a member of an organization that requires teamwork for success? It isn't much different from how a team of horses pulls together. If you are a member of a team, or thinking about joining one, step back a moment and reflect upon your role. For a team to work well together, older members need to mentor younger members. Younger members also need to be open to feedback from the veterans. Unity as the ultimate goal is also important. When a team of horses pulls together, one individual horse usually doesn't stick out in comparison with the other horses. In the same way with teams, when whole units pull together and move forward in unison, it really is like an effective symphony that has the instrumental players fulfilling their individual roles.

In the same way that wise older horses tolerate younger, soon to be stronger horses, veteran team members need to be tolerant of younger team members. Veteran team members should provide key leadership, emotional stability in word and deed, and a centered mission focus. Younger team members can provide needed new ideas, an enthusiasm that may bolster a healthy competitive spirit, and a willingness to challenge others. Maintaining the status quo is unacceptable and change must occur for the team to succeed.

The closing part of the Scripture verse appears out of place but it really isn't. The gentleman driving the team of horses blurts out that "Babylon has fallen . . . . All the images of its gods lie shattered on the ground." The Bible often talks about the idols we human beings create. Idols that adversely affect teamwork can include self-aggrandizement and the pursuit of personal glory – a far cry from giving God the glory.

Prayer: Lord, thank you for allowing us to fulfill roles on the teams to which you have called us. Amen.

Then the end will come, when he hands over the kingdom to God the Father after he has destroyed all dominion, authority and power.
1 Corinthians 15:24

DOMINION AND CO-CREATION

The word "kingdom" is used 347 times in the NIV's translation of the Bible. Many of those instances refer to Christ's rule subsequent to his second coming. Others refer to this current time as living in God's kingdom, which is not yet perfected, but will be perfected, upon his eternal redemption during the consummation. The above Scripture verse points out that Christ will hand off the kingdom to God the Father after he has destroyed all dominion, authority, and power. I've often wondered what the kingdom will look like when dominion, authority, and power are destroyed.

The kingdom of God during the end times will be evidenced by Christ conquering all. Regarding this specific aspect of Christ having complete dominion, my mom used to frequently say, "Son, the kingdom of God is at hand." I would say in response, "What do you mean when you say this?"

She would then go into an explanation that trials and tribulations are only temporary and regardless of these challenges, we must do our part to cultivate God's kingdom here on earth. She would then further describe the cultural mandate of dominion and co-creation.

Dominion and co-creation – those two words have so many connotations. Genesis 1:26 cites it this way, "Then God said, 'Let us make mankind in our image, in our likeness, so that they may rule over the fish in the sea and the birds in the sky, over the livestock and all the wild animals, and over all the creatures that move along the ground." God encouraged man to rule over all creatures and to have dominion over the earth. We have been instructed to co-create and "do well" with God's kingdom.

The kingdom of God referenced here is realized when dominion, power, and authority are minimized and Christ-likeness is maximized. In looking at these three words, what does the opposite mean in each case? The opposite of dominion is not to have a domain (not to control). The antithesis of power is lack of influence or lack of supreme rule over an individual. The antonym of authority is powerlessness and not to have a say-so over an individual. So, Christ-likeness looks like freedom without bondage, supervision without power, and allowing God to rule rather than man.

These qualities in turn are an invitation to embody God's grace to us through our actions. Grace lived out in everyday life includes a willingness to influence others positively rather than trying to control them. Grace in our life includes giving a friend or family member guidance without resorting to imperatives. Grace also means that one should be willing to instruct without being patronizing. Some might say in the everyday world of "push and shove," this approach is too "soft" and that whoever leads with grace lacks a backbone. Thankfully, there are some individuals that believe co-creating in this manner is the way we are called to live our everyday life of Christ-likeness.

How about you? Have you reflected upon how you can extend Christ-likeness today? Perhaps this includes being willing to respond with a kind word instead of a quick verbal jab. Possibly this means just listening to a friend who is in dire need, without providing a quick and easy answer. For others, living in this way will involve affirming someone's strengths and gently suggesting ways in which they might already be equipped to image our Creator more. Approach each day in the spirit of seeking to serve in God's kingdom here on earth.

Prayer: Today Lord help us to bring kingdom values to our everyday lives by helping us to lead with kindness, gentle instruction, and balanced truth. We want to be your instrument of co-creation. Amen.

> But the fruit of the Spirit is love, joy, peace, forbearance, kindness, goodness, faithfulness, gentleness and self-control. Against such things there is no law. Galatians 5:22–23

AUTHENTIC COMMITMENT

The unsung hero of our family was my father. The depth of his faithfulness was immeasurable. Dad would dress mom every day. When he wasn't at work, he would load mom in and out of the car, taker her to zillions of the kids' activities, take her to the hospital, and feed her at dinner after coming home from work. He never delegated that task although I do remember mom getting famished at times waiting for the next bite!

How do we humans "put on" love, joy, peace, forbearance, kindness, goodness, faithfulness, gentleness, and self-control? The answer is that the Holy Spirit must manifest these qualities in us. We are unable to realistically take on these traits, unless the Holy Spirit is allowed to actively grow these traits in our personal lives.

The one characteristic that continues to be front and center in this verse is faithfulness. Faithfulness is authentic commitment. As you look over the fruits of the Spirit, which ones do you want to have the Holy Spirit produce at a greater depth in the days, weeks, and months ahead? As I look back at my childhood, I see that the fruit of the Spirit was produced in my father through his trials.

My father's fruit of the Spirit included the following:
- Love – a willingness to raise seven children with a depth of care that was fair and grace-filled.
- Joy – enduring the tedious daily challenges of routine tasks with a smile and positive attitude.
- Peace – keeping a "shalom" in the home by focusing on God's Word and a weekly Sabbath rest.
- Forbearance – asking for forgiveness and seeking forgiveness when everyone was tired and patience levels were running short.
- Kindness – living each day with an attitude of generosity and simple gestures of please, thank you, and speaking thoughtfully to others.

- Goodness – reaching out to unwed mothers and helping them with their insurance and personal needs before their baby was born.
- Faithfulness – an authentic commitment to a disabled spouse and to seven children through trying times.
- Gentleness – instead of acting as the world does with insistence, demands, and a boisterous voice, choosing the alternative of a soft-spoken problem-solving approach.
- Self-Control – demonstrating discipline in habits, living life in moderation, being willing to do without material things because of a willingness to live simply.

I've often wondered how my father was so authentically committed to his wife and family during the twenty-four years of her illness. It has become clear to me that he was asking the Holy Spirit to grow the fruit of the Spirit in him. Essentially, he was dying to self and was living out Christ's greatest two commandments of loving God and loving his neighbors.

Prayer: Lord, help us to turn away from the self-effort of trying to obtain the fruit of the Spirit ourselves. Give us a willingness to have you transform us through your Holy Spirit. Help us to grow in the development of authentic commitment as we strive to be closer to you. May it be so, Lord. Amen.

"This, then, is how you should pray: 'Our Father in heaven, hallowed be your name, your kingdom come, your will be done, on earth as it is in heaven.'" Matthew 6:9–10

How Does God Answer Prayer

For many, prayer is one of the toughest topics to write or talk about. Although what I have to share here is deeply personal, I do so not with an air of piety but mean it to be merely descriptive. Throughout the twenty-four years my mother had M.S., she was often grasping for healing or treatments that would slow the progression of the disease. She would see various doctors to verify the diagnosis. She was willing to try any type of treatment. She once endured ice baths to reduce the internal core temperature of her body. It was brutal to watch these ice bath treatments, and it was even more brutal to watch her body temperature warm up after being in a tub of ice cubes for 45 minutes.

Fast forward twenty-five years later, after my mom's passing. My wife now has M.S. She, too, is grasping for treatment regimens and alternative options for slowing the progression of her disease. Recently she received news that she is experiencing a relapse. This was somewhat anticipated because she has had to change from the most effective M.S. drug treatment to another treatment due to a brain virus positive test. In the past five years, she has tried many alternatives. Some alternatives have included a gluten-free diet, Avonex (an interferon weekly drug treatment), Tysabri (an amazingly effective once a month intravenous treatment), herbal supplements, lower ph alkaline-type powders, and a few others that likely help as vitamin additives but carry little guarantee for a long-term positive prognosis.

The treatment stories of my mother and my wife illustrate how easily we can become drawn into a situation and potentially lose focus on how to pray. How do we regain our focus? The verse above guides us to pray with an acknowledgement of God ruling in heaven and to honor his holy name. Then the verse challenges us to call on God's kingdom coming to earth, and that we will be accepting of his will on earth as it is in heaven.

The last portion of this Scripture verse, "your will be done, on earth as it is in heaven" is where I've seen miracles in my mother's life and in that of my wife. The answers to prayer have first included a change in their attitude. They both had a spirit of praise evident in their lives. Second, they honored God in their hearts and actions. I've also seen them acknowledge his holiness (hallowedness) and the promise of his kingdom. Both of these women were aware not only of his kingdom that will come when Christ reigns in a new heaven and earth, but also that his kingdom was and is ruling presently in their hearts.

Acceptance of "your will be done, on earth as it is in heaven" is easier said than done. Obeying God's will is the key step. Can you imagine being accepting of a disease that is degrading your body more and more each day? It is only possible by the sequence described in this prayer. First, we must have an attitude of knowing God is in control (he is ruling). Secondly, we should be honoring him in all we say and do. Thirdly, we are to take a long-term kingdom approach and anticipate there will be a time of full redemption. Lastly, we are to pray that God's will is accomplished in the same way on earth that it is in heaven. This is the miracle of faith.

Prayer: God, change our attitude, challenge us to honor you instead of the daily idols that can develop in our life, help us anticipate your reign in a new heaven and earth, and lastly help us accept your will. Give us a spirit of prayer like this. Amen.

Now the Berean Jews were of more noble character than those in Thessalonica, for they received the message with great eagerness and examined the Scriptures every day to see if what Paul said was true. Acts 17:11

THE CHARACTER OF GOD

One of my siblings mentioned that the character of God was evident in our parents' lives in many ways. What does the word "character" entail? Synonyms for the word character include nature, appearance, attributes, reputation, emotions, habits, or complexion. These synonyms, however, don't seem to come close to what Acts 17:11 was referring to when describing the Bereans as being of "noble character."

The Bereans referred to in this Scripture were willing to compare real life choices with what Paul was teaching. It even sounds like the Bereans were consistently evaluating what was being taught as compared to what was found in Scripture. Being willing to examine your life choices in light of Scripture is how noble character develops according to the Bereans.

I can attest to the fact that my mom received the message of Scripture eagerly. In addition, she examined the Scriptures every day in the same way the Bereans were daily checking up on Paul's instruction.

The biggest challenge of developing noble character by applying this verse involves the regimen of consuming Scripture "daily." Yes, it says that every day the Bereans were verifying if what Paul said was true. However, there are so many distractions in life. These distractions prevent us from digging into the Word of God. If we ask ourselves honestly, we might see the lack of sleep, too few margins built into our days, lack of discipline, complex work schedules, digital addictions, unhealthy habits, family dynamics, and more as examples of these distractions.

Noble character is developed by allowing God's grace to speak to us during the time we set aside for Scripture study. How do we push away some of the distractions above and dig into the gift of the Word? Habit-forming disciplines include designating a set time of the day to daily examine God's Word, building time margins into your schedule, consuming devotional reading materials that are rooted in Scripture, preparing for sermons you will hear by studying the Scripture ahead of time, and evaluating and applying what you have heard from the pulpit in the context of Scripture.

When you meet a person of noble character, their "character" often shines through because they are "centered" in God's Word. They are applying God's Word on a daily basis. They worry less about self and more about others. They live lives of giving God the glory and deflecting credit to others. I'm personally grateful for my parents also because they prioritized the development of God's character and let this habit in turn shape their family's priorities. Without this eagerness to learn, how are we supposed to live with noble character? Our tendency to be self-reliant will lead to an inadequate attempt to live out the character of God. How about you? Are you willing to dig into his Word on a daily basis?

Prayer: God, forgive us when we fall short in examining your Word. Call us to hear your instruction with positive anticipation and true openness. Please bring individuals into our lives that model noble character so we can learn their disciplines and habits. Give us a willingness to examine our margins of life so we can adjust our priorities to be closer to you. Thank you for calling us back to center. Amen.

Do not eat the food of a begrudging host, do not crave his delicacies; for he is the kind of person who is always thinking about the cost. "Eat and drink," he says to you, but his heart is not with you. You will vomit up the little you have eaten and will have wasted your compliments. Proverbs 23:6–8

GRACIOUS HOSPITALITY

Have you ever been hosted by someone when the experience included a glimmer of meeting with an angel? Gracious hospitality includes the quality of food being secondary in comparison with the conversation and atmosphere. Being welcoming and hospitable was a priority for my mother. In the Proverbs 23 scripture above, we are essentially guided to avoid being a begrudging host and think less about the costs of what we are sharing. The Scripture challenges us to make sure our hearts are in the right place. Lastly, the verse cautions about not wasting compliments after being with a begrudging host.

"Do not forget to show hospitality to strangers, for by so doing some people have shown hospitality to angels without knowing it" (Hebrews 13:2) guides us further on how we are supposed to be hospitable. My mom consistently had the gift of being hospitable to strangers. Picture the dynamics of a dinner table that was set up for seven children, two parents, an unwed mother and most often an additional stranger or two. Rarely did we have extravagant food. Consistently my dad had to do "portion control" as the food was distributed. However, the interpersonal interaction of the seven children was dynamic. The conversation was by far the most important activity of the evening activities and meal.

The trait and practice of hospitality is one of the gifts we are all called to share as servant leaders, but we don't all easily practice hospitality. What keeps us from practicing hospitality?

- Being too busy with everyday life
- An aversion to meeting new people
- Sense of inferiority in hosting others
- Perception of not having enough food or resources
- Limiting the number of personal friends and acquaintanc-

es

The list could go on. But regardless of our aversions or insecurities, Scripture calls us to show hospitality to others. Let go of perfection because it can be the worst enemy of good. Avoid craving delicacies. Find a way to share sincere compliments. Make your best effort to go out of your way and accommodate strangers. Some of the most rewarding experiences in our family's life included what transpired after we hosted someone around our dinner table. Those "strangers" became spouses, a future teacher of many of the children, a lifetime friend, and one of these strangers even became the most influential individual in the lives of the four youngest children.

The cost of being in relationship with others is well worth the investment. Reprioritize your calendar. Find a way to say hello to a stranger at church. Invite someone new into your life. Nudge yourself out of your comfort zone and slow down to make a difference by hosting someone you don't know very well. Whether it is a friend of one of your kids, a parent from down the street, or an individual you met at a recent meeting, ask God to reveal who you can host around your table.

Prayer: Lord, help us reprioritize our lives. Walk with us as we work at slowing down and aim for greater balance. Help us to share kind words with others. May our ways not begrudge others. Fill us with a spirit of generous hospitality that moves us to open our doors even to those we don't know well. Thank you for bringing angels into our lives on a daily basis. Amen.

"If anyone causes one of these little ones – those who believe in me – to stumble, it would be better for them to have a large millstone hung around their neck and to be drowned in the depths of the sea." Matthew 18:6

What Do You Do When You Stumble and Fall?

My mother stumbled and fell more times than I can count. She fell on the ground when the children tried to move her. Unsuccessful transfers caused her to fall when we tried to:

- relocate her from the car to the wheelchair or wheelchair to the car;
- transfer her from the wheelchair to her hospital bed located in the front room;
- lift her from the bathroom to the wheelchair;
- move her up the stairs and come crashing down the stairs.

The list could go on. Many of these falls were harmless because mom's body was so relaxed that she couldn't tense her muscles. Sometimes though, the tumbles caused bruising and cuts. Thankfully, none of these falls involved an immediate hospital visit.

What I remember are my mom's responses to these kinds of accidents. Most often, she just started laughing so hard that no one involved in the "crash and burn" event could take their responsibility for dropping her too seriously. The second result of our "stumbling" was that neighbors regularly came to our rescue. Finally, we children realized that we had dropped mom because we were trying to lift her without another sibling helping and because we lacked strength and proper form (using our legs and locking our knees before the transfer occurred).

My mother lived out Job 4:4 "Your words have supported those who stumbled, you have strengthened faltering knees." How did her responses to being dropped positively influence her "little ones"? First of all, she kept her composure. She laughed and kept the spirits of the situation fairly light (unless it was brutally cold out with snow on the ground). Secondly, she calmly stayed prone on the ground and instructed us to go find a neighbor to help. Thirdly, while waiting for help, she prayed. Fourthly, she instructed us on how to get out of the mess we just got ourselves in because we were careless or lacked proven mechanics that had previously been used time and again.

There are some deep lessons in this experience. What do you do when you stumble? I'm sure there are times when you respond in anger. Other times you may respond in bitterness and resentment and blame it on someone else. Indeed, "little ones" observe your reactions more than you think when you stumble. Children also observe responses of composure and taking the time to pray versus over-reacting. Regardless of the circumstances, getting right back up with more determination than ever was my mother's final response to stumbling. Plenty of life lessons were observed when we dropped mom on the ground.

Prayer: Lord, forgive us when we respond inappropriately to our stumbling. Guide us to better mentor our children and the youth we influence. Help us to acknowledge the importance of appropriate responses. Amen.

"Blessed are the poor in spirit, for theirs is the kingdom of heaven. Blessed are those who mourn, for they will be comforted. Blessed are the meek, for they will inherit the earth." Matthew 5:3–5

EMPATHY AND COMPASSION

One of my siblings said that mom really poured-on compassion. She was so good at it that her compassion was "better than any type of candy." That is saying a lot because most children really, really like candy. To encourage children more with compassion than with candy is commendable. The Scripture verse here guides us in skills of empathy and compassion. We are called to be modest in our spirit. We are called to be understanding of those who are mourning. It is possible to inherit the kingdom of God here on earth if we demonstrate meekness. Synonyms of "meek" include humble, timid, gentle, submissive, modest, compliant, and mild. These qualities are not what the world considers to be "appropriate" characteristics. But they are characteristics of Jesus instruction for us.

How can one possess empathy and compassion in the hustle and bustle of the world we live in today? Living out intentional and strong interpersonal skills is a way of putting on compassion and empathy. The absolutely only way to live out meekness is to slow down and express a personal interest in someone else. My mom was a master at trying to understand others. She enrolled each of her children in Empathy 100. She constantly demanded an attitude of humility by expecting us to:

- Say please and thank you when you ask for or receive something from someone.
- Look someone in the eyes when you meet them and ask about their personal background.
- Gently correct and guide others instead of yelling and screaming at them.
- When you have wronged someone, humbly approach them and ask them to forgive your shortcomings.
- Submit to others, and, at work, acknowledge that you are responsible to someone else.
- Be modest in your accomplishments and think of others

as better than yourself.

- When requesting something, do so mildly rather than being overly demanding.
- Choose a spirit of complimenting others in your work and home assignments.

To live out an empathetic and compassionate lifestyle is counter-cultural. Many modern cultural contexts often indicate that it is better to demand something versus saying please or thank you. Insisting on being heard rather than expressing an interest in someone is culturally acceptable. Speaking to someone out of love, rather than berating them, is often considered abnormal behavior. Living in humility runs counter to the standard practice of proudly discussing one's personal and professional accomplishments. Submissiveness is now considered a character trait of weakness because the world expects "effective" leaders to be domineering. Modesty is a lost art in a culture that now reinforces "boldness" and "assertiveness" no matter the circumstances. Soft-spoken approaches to negotiation are heard of less and less because flashy is the new savvy. Compliance in spirit and working with others in a spirit of collaboration vs. command is a rare practice.

These sorts of empathetic characteristics are possible but not commonly used. In your day, week, and upcoming months, try out the "soft" compassionate approach to see if this balance can help you in your personal and professional relationships. We all possess hard skills (technical) and soft skills (interpersonal skills). Consciously leaning into empathetic and compassionate skills is a way to live out Scripture. Be countercultural and live out Jesus' words in these beatitudes.

Prayer: Lord, help us to express more interest in others' personal lives. Forgive us when we lack empathy and compassion. Guide us somehow to take the focus off ourselves and shift this to others. Amen.

Love Those Who Have Wronged You

When I asked my siblings the key lessons they learned from an influential parent plagued by hardship, their most memorable teachings of childhood included:

- Love covers over a multitude of sins.
- Even while we were yet sinners, Christ died for us.
- You can love your enemies.
- People are valuable, oh so valuable.
- It was easy to remember being loved as a child.

Mom talked with us often about being a "giver" or a "taker." Hearing it described today using the analogy of water, one would likely say a bucket-dipper or a bucket-filler. Another might compare it to seeing a glass as half-full or half-empty. We learned these lessons through modeling. In the early years of M.S., mom would model giving vs. taking every day. When the unwed mothers were overwhelmed with their impending delivery of an unexpected child, she encouraged them with timely compliments. At times, some of these unwed mothers would take on a mean streak and become adversarial with family members. Mom would look into their eyes and softly extend words of grace and guidance. In these words, there would be correction, re-direction, and amazing bits of encouragement.

As the journey of life brings about unexpected bumps and bruises, how should one respond to the "enemies" that somehow appear? Very few people wake up in the morning planning to irritate someone else. But enemies can develop when harsh words are shared, jealousies surface, and attitudes lean towards negativity. In addition, our humanness can be so easily entangled with petty righteousness and what others owe us.

Learning to love unconditionally is a powerful bucket-filler. Time and again observing love in action helped us to not hold onto material or experiences as the ultimate end. Watching mom nurture our helpers from the depths of sin to valued human beings created in his image was amazing. People are valuable and mom somehow, instead of seeing them as enemies, saw these individuals as image bearers in God's kingdom. The world would be an amazing place if each of us saw sinful but forgiven people as having promise. The modeling action that caught the eye of each child was her willingness to do "good" to others without expecting anything in return. Smiles, kind words, an undemanding spirit, compliments and constructive comments were the norm of the day. Love in action and attitude is a potent memory.

Prayer: Lord, teach us to be able to better love all those around us. Guide us in learning to give versus taking as an eternal lesson that can help shape our lives. As we experience the rough edges of those with whom we come in contact, guide us in kindness in doing good to them. Please also give us a spirit of reflection before we respond, because humanly we are unable to respond this way. Nudge us to give ourselves away. Challenge us to give our whole being away too, so we can accomplish your purposes. Thank you for the models we have in our lives that love their enemies and give without expecting anything in return. Amen.

> . . . put on the new self, which is being renewed in knowledge in the image of its Creator. Colossians 3:10

CREATED IN THE IMAGE OF GOD

Putting on the new self brings so many thoughts into our limited feeble minds. We were created to abide in God's Word and live in the image of the Creator. How to live in the image of the Creator is the challenge of this verse. The middle portion of this verse calls us to be renewed in knowledge. In addition to observing the creation and the master's touch in this creation, one clear way to be renewed in this knowledge is found in James 1:23–24, which says, "Anyone who listens to the word but does not do what it says is like someone who looks at his face in a mirror and, after looking at himself, goes away and immediately forgets what he looks like."

Scripture is our guidebook for being renewed in knowledge in the image of its Creator. I understand this Scripture in James to say that initially we see in a mirror dimly, but as we grow in the knowledge of Jesus Christ and Scripture, we see more clearly in the mirror how to put on the new self.

Watching two close family members battle a disease has caused me to reflect on how to put on a new self. I've found comfort in viewing both of these scriptures in Colossians and James. My mom's circumstances, and now those of my wife, have drawn me closer to the Creator. Frankly, I've asked "Why?" many times. Why me? Why is it necessary to have so much disease around our lives? Why so much pain? Why are there so many people affected by this debilitating and progressive virus called Multiple Sclerosis? I've come to the conclusion that it isn't about me. All of these challenges have pointed me to the Creator – although you may find our comfort somewhat strange to comprehend.

The comfort I've found through these circumstances is that I'm not my own. My mom was not her own. My wife is not her own. Mom's perspective on this screamed the loudest. She often said that "whatever you do, do for the glory of God." Putting on a new self for her was making the most of each and every situation. Mom guided me in my emotions and reactions. She didn't allow anger or bitterness to build in her because of a calling to put on a new self. Mom thrived on the promise that we were created in his image and, someday, we will all be healed. She found solace in the knowledge of Scripture; and this opportunity to learn more about the Creator and experience his creation in simple ways was mom's daily foundational strength. She just didn't allow circumstances to dictate her happiness.

How about you? Do circumstances dictate your life or do you delve into God's Word, seek the knowledge of the Creator, and see in a mirror more clearly how to conduct your life in a Christ-like manner? All of this is so much easier said than done. Sin in our lives and all around us tempts us to dwell on circumstances. Even a larger temptation is to look at other families and assume that their situations are so much easier than our own! Mom did not let that happen to us. Anytime we used the term, "I wish" you were healthy, or "I wish" you could walk normally, or similar thoughts, mom brought us back to reality. She would re-direct each child back to the importance of seeking the image of our Creator. By this measure, no family has normal or better circumstances. No matter our family situation, we are called to put on a new self, grow in the knowledge of Scripture, and see each of our fellow human beings as being created in his image. The opportunities are limitless with this perspective. Learning how to focus on God as creator and doing what the Word of God calls us to do is a better way to live than coveting another person's circumstances.

Prayer: Lord, help us to focus on your image. Renew us through the knowledge of your Word. Call us to put on a new self that reflects Christlikeness. Move us from looking at others to looking at you. Amen.

. . . the day of the Lord will come like a thief. The heavens will disappear with a roar; the elements will be destroyed by fire, and the earth and everything in it will be laid bare. Since everything will be destroyed in this way, what kind of people ought you to be? You ought to live holy and godly lives as you look forward to the day of God and speed its coming. That day will bring about the destruction of the heavens by fire, and the elements will melt in the heat. But in keeping with his promise we are looking forward to a new heaven and a new earth, where righteousness dwells. 2 Peter 3:10–13

ALREADY BUT NOT YET

We live in God's kingdom here on earth, but we also have a promise of Christ's return where a new heaven and new earth will be revealed. Mom frequently stood on God's promises in these verses. She would weep about her current body's state, but in the next breath, she would rejoice about how she looked forward to Christ's return and the opportunity to experience the new heaven and new earth. Through this Scripture verse, mom often talked to family, friends, and neighbors about how important it is to live blamelessly in this "already" time period, but loosely hold onto earthly items because we have "not yet" experienced the fullness of the new earth.

Have you ever contemplated your responsibility to live where righteousness dwells? My mom was an agent of reconciliation and in this way she modeled a place where righteousness dwelled. She attempted to live a holy and blameless life. With seven children, she was consistently seeking peace and living well in spite of her circumstances. She challenged her children to live out their time here on earth with a heavenly perspective. Included in this perspective of living was an effort to encourage a dominion over the earth. She regularly talked about our responsibility to subdue the earth and "co-create" all that we could. Co-creation means doing our part to strive towards the new heaven and new earth while at the same time acknowledging that we are not yet to the point of full reconciliation and subsequent consummation.

As children, we were challenged to live holy and blameless. We fell short plenty of times with this charge, but we consistently saw model parents make the most of nearly impossible circumstances. These circumstances of fire shaped siblings who are presently serving as a teacher for the U.S. Center for World Missions, a pastor of the same church for the past fifteen years, a senior executive for the nonprofit parachurch organization Outreach, a senior administrator in Christian education, a cardiac care nurse, a contractor bid relations liaison, and an international photographer.

These "callings" have taken each of the children to serve in various professions. We were asked often by mom the question in this verse. "What kind of people ought you to be?" She would challenge us live holy and Godly lives as we looked forward to the day of God and speed its coming. As individuals created in his image, we attempted to live up to this charge, but we also acknowledged that any effort to strive towards the new heaven and new earth paled in comparison to God's sovereign guidance. Time and again, mom challenged us further to "do what we can" to serve in God's kingdom here on earth but also to acknowledge fully that we are instruments of God's divine plan. Living well by holding loosely onto earthly pursuits has allowed our family to give ourselves away in personal and professional pursuits. God promises a new heaven and a new earth. Until that time, we should strive to fulfill our responsibility to subdue the earth and live righteously in all aspects of our earthly calling.

Prayer: Lord, we want to make disciples of men and subdue the earth, but we also anticipate a new heaven and earth. Help us to balance this tension and live holy and blameless lives. Give us models and help us to mentor others to prepare for the new heaven and earth. Amen.

Jesus replied, "No one who puts a hand to the plow and looks back is fit for service in the kingdom of God." Luke 9:62

LOOKING AWAY FROM "IF ONLY . . ."

If only I had done this. If only I had done that . . . things would have been different. It is so easy to look back. Is hindsight always easier than foresight? As humans, I really believe we are inclined to look back at the past and wish things were different. Even with the awful side effects of M.S., I never heard my mom say, "I wish this disease never happened." Bravely, she seldom looked back at the plow rows. It could have been easy for her to ask for the cup to be removed each and every day.

She faced daily challenges, including an inability to walk normally, imbalance, near-immediate loss of her voice, inability to feed herself, loss of independence to use the bathroom, inability to complete daily hygiene activities such as brushing her teeth, combing hair, dressing herself, and perhaps most of all, just being unable live independently day by day.

Psychologically, with the initial diagnosis, my mom had to battle forms of depression and essentially went through stages of coping with grief. Denial, anger, bargaining, depression, and acceptance were all part of dealing with the disease. The sooner she stopped looking back, the sooner she was able to move into kingdom work. There were many individuals that positively influenced mom to avoid looking back at plow rows. Neighbors encouraged her by stopping by frequently. Family stood by her through thick and thin. Her spouse was tough on the inside but compassionate on the outside. School families were accepting of our family shortcomings and many of these families brought us into their community circle. Kingdom work was a part of mom's daily living after she accepted her circumstances. Some of this "Kingdom of God" work included ministering to unwed mothers on a daily basis, praying for many friends and family, and modeling contentment regardless of her circumstances. Many would say, after visiting mom and observing her countenance, that they just experienced one of their most inspiring days of their life.

Today, my wife also faces choices of looking back at the plow rows or considering the opportunity to serve in the kingdom of God. Her daily challenges include an inability to navigate uneven surfaces, feeling numbness in fingers and hands, stresses of coordinating the buttoning of a shirt, taking extensive time to tie one's shoes, being unable to project her voice, and periodically coughing violently without explanation. Add on the daily challenge and frustrations of trying to walk with someone and pace herself in the same steps as others.

Self-doubt, depression, dealing with a new normal, adjusting to the thought of being incapacitated, comparing oneself to her former self tempted her to look back at the plow rows. At the start of the disease, she asked herself such questions as, "Does God hear me, does he care, will he heal me, and will he help me deal with my circumstances?" Thankfully, after approximately two years, the disposition of my wife shifted from looking back at the plow rows to kingdom work. Without going into too much detail and risking the perception of inappropriate pride, she invests in others rather than just focusing on herself. Thankfully, she accepts her circumstances and doesn't look back at the plow rows very often.

Prayer: Lord, thank you for your guidance and encouragement to avoid dwelling on the past. Challenge us to serve others in the kingdom. Help us to move away from focusing on ourselves and call us to do your kingdom work. Guide us to make a difference in being content regardless of our circumstances. Amen.

> The Son is the image of the invisible God, the firstborn over all creation. For in him all things were created: things in heaven and on earth, visible and invisible, whether thrones or powers or rulers or authorities; all things have been created through him and for him. He is before all things, and in him all things hold together. Colossians 1:15–17

HE WHO HOLDS ALL THINGS TOGETHER

Despite my mother's challenges with Multiple Sclerosis, she challenged me to be confident in how God miraculously holds all things, including our bodies, together. Furthermore, she drew me into the sciences because of the amazing way God created the human body with such simple physics as mechanical advantage and dynamics of movement. For instance, after watching how fast the body can degrade, I was drawn to study the anatomy and physiology of the human body. In less than one calendar year, at the age of 31, my mother's muscular function deteriorated from normal walking, to using a cane, to a walker, and then to a wheelchair. The experience provoked me in a good way to be captivated with the study of the human body.

In the midst of this experience, there were seven children in our home, of which the youngest two children were twins under the age of one. Due to the debilitating effects of M.S., my mother was never able to hold her infant twins because of the extreme risk of dropping the infants. Observing this family situation drew me to the sciences and caused me to dig deeper into investigating how all things hold together. In the midst of this family crisis, my father came up with a mastermind of an idea to influence culture and to hold all things together in our household. My father determined that as a family we were going to honor how all things have been created through the Son of God and for him. He decided that we could make it through this family crisis of seven children in our home under the age of ten by embracing unwed mothers, and in turn having them help take care of the needs of his wife and children.

This Colossians scripture verse highlights that the Son is the invisible image of God and the firstborn over all creation. Then the Scripture further explains that all things were created in him and for him. Accepting this is easier said than done. As my mother physically continued to degrade, my interest in physics expanded even further. I became enthralled with mechanical advantages and movement. At the age of ten, it became a daily responsibility for me to move my mother from her wheelchair to her hospital bed or vice versa from her hospital bed to her wheelchair so she could be transported to and from the car. This was no easy task of mechanical advantage. Mom's Rozendal Dutch heritage was evident in her large-boned nearly six-foot frame. A five-foot-tall ten-year-old lifting a six-foot-tall mother was only possible with the physics of locking knees, lifting with core abdominal strength, and cooperating with equal and opposite directional movements. Needless to say, thirty-two feet per second also applies when you drop your mother accidentally to the ground. We tried to slow down the acceleration when mishaps occurred, but most of the time it just happened too fast.

This verse closes "he is before all things and in him all things hold together." With God holding all things together, our family had amazing experiences managing my mother's M.S. In twenty-four years, we hosted fifty-five individuals in our home that took care of the family. Most of these individuals decided to forego an abortion and allow God to hold all things together in their own lives. We saw the miracle of infant births transpire first-hand many times. It was an honor to hold each of these newborns and nurture them in their first months of God's creation. Now, as a fast forward, I have the privilege of observing how God holds all things together with my wife's M.S. I look back on my unique childhood experiences and am grateful God "held all things together" to prepare me for my wife's battle with M.S.

Prayer: Lord, thank you for promising that you are before all things and you hold them together. Amen.

He came and preached peace to you who were far away and peace to those who were near. For through him we both have access to the Father by one Spirit. Consequently, you are no longer foreigners and strangers, but fellow citizens with God's people and also members of his household, built on the foundation of the apostles and prophets, with Christ Jesus himself as the chief cornerstone. In him the whole building is joined together and rises to become a holy temple in the Lord. And in him you too are being built together to become a dwelling in which God lives by his Spirit. Ephesians 2:17–22

RE-CENTERING ON THE CORNERSTONE

The Christmas season can be such a "re-centering" time for families. I've often wondered why it takes a certain time of the year to bring us back to a balanced life. Ephesians 2 guides us in finding a balance because this scripture first talks about Jesus as being our peace ("center"). He reconciled the sacred and the secular by sacrificially giving of himself. Through this, we are provided access to the Father, Son, and Holy Spirit. Paul then explains that we are fellow citizens with God's people, members of his household that is built on the foundation of the apostles, with Christ as the chief ("center") cornerstone.

How is it possible to daily live out peace, reconciliation, wholeness, the Trinity, citizenship, and Christ as the "center" of our lives? One way is to ask yourself: who or what is the center of my life? For example, while growing up in the city of Denver, we had a Christmas tradition that challenged our family to return to "center" by bringing the whole family together for a worship experience. One day a year, around Christmastime, our family of nine (seven siblings and two parents) would "re-center" together by singing Christmas carols in the basement where the piano was located. This was much harder than one may think because our mother was bedridden. We would place her in a wheelchair and take her down twelve stairs. We usually didn't crash the wheelchair. Upon arrival in the basement, we would place the current newborn sibling or single mother's baby in the bassinet. Every member of the family was required to participate in singing Christmas carols in a basement sing-a-long. This truly was a time to "center" and reflect upon the peace and chief cornerstone we have in Jesus Christ.

In the hustle and bustle of life, including Christmastime, is there a reason why it is so easy to get off-center? I'm convinced we lose our "center" because we try to substitute, throughout the year, inappropriate or ineffective cornerstones. During the holidays, we tend toward: overscheduling our days and evenings, the pursuit of happiness through materialism, self-sufficiency, overindulgence, or a focus on self vs. others. All of these are pushes and tugs that are contrary to the Spirit and illustrations of how we let sin creep into our lives.

I'd like to challenge you this Christmas season to simplify your life. Make Christ your chief cornerstone. Sing Christmas carols with your family. Stop and "re-center" by being willing to allow God to redeem key foundations of your life. Try to point towards the New Year by setting specific goals for the liturgies of your heart and mind. Establish new habits for acknowledging that Christ must be the cornerstone of every aspect of your life. Through acknowledging Christ as cornerstone, God will be glorified.

Prayer: Father, forgive us when we try to find peace by separating you from certain aspects of our life. Redeem our habits, Lord, so we can live as whole beings and be guided by your Spirit in all aspects of our words, thoughts, and deeds. During Christmas and next year, "center" us by being our chief cornerstone. Amen.

A person's wisdom yields patience; it is to one's glory to overlook an offense. A king's rage is like the roar of a lion, but his favor is like dew on the grass. Proverbs 19:11–12

Be joyful in hope, patient in affliction, faithful in prayer. Romans 12:12

DEMONSTRATING PATIENCE

Patience is something very few people are born with. Thirty years after my mother's extended battle with Multiple Sclerosis, my spouse now has had M.S. for six years. Picture this scene around the dinner table. Everyone is working to set the table and place the food on the dinner table. A complication arises when your spouse who is carrying food over to the table loses her muscular control and drops the main dish on the floor. Now you have a clear choice on demonstrating patience. Do you let out an "Oh no!" or ask hard questions like, "What is wrong with you?" or do you seek to say, "I'm sorry, let me clean this up. Everything will be okay"?

Proverbs 19:11 clearly states that we are to overlook an offense. It also points out that rage is overrated compared to being in favor with someone. Deeper than all of this is the scriptural guidance that we live to God's glory when we overlook an offense. Oh, it is so easy to talk about a depth of love, but much, much tougher in reality to obey this type of command.

Revisit a scene that happens often in our home. Everyone wants to live a normal life but sometimes that just isn't possible. Normally, one would prepare a meal and at or about dinner time, the food would make it over to the table without incident. Normally, that doesn't happen in our home. At some point in the set-up for dinner, food or silverware or seasonings that are being moved from countertop to the dining area end up on the floor. Alternatives for responding are quite clear. Respond in a form of rage, or respond in patience as described in the Scripture.

Romans 12:12 is a complementary scripture that guides us to infuse a Christian perspective on kingdom service into all we do. First of all, we are supposed to live in hope. This means we should live with the words please and thanks on our tongues often. We are to bless others as often as possible. We are called to avoid retaliation and to take the high road. Secondly, after we demonstrate joyful hope, we are to be patient in affliction. Hope is first. Patience is the second command. Why in this order? Hope leads into patience. Dinner will be served regardless of what gets dropped on the floor before the meal begins. Affliction will occur but all is okay because we can live joyfully because of hope.

Being faithful in prayer is the anchor of our actions in living for the Lord. Being faithful in prayer and thinking of others before your self is an important component of patience. Joy, hope, patience, faithfulness, and prayer: all tall orders for fallen people. There are days when I often fall short of these commands, but I'm trying to live out an obedient life. One day at a time, we are called to clean up whatever we drop on the floor or to reach out to whoever needs help in their affliction. Nobody really lives a normal life because we all experience some form of affliction. Ask God today to help you demonstrate a depth of patience.

Prayer: Thank you Lord for the challenges you bring to help us mature in patience. Whether it is an affliction that others know about or not, guide us in living a joyful life, help us to share hope with others, to be patient in suffering, and to be faithful through it all. Call us to be consistently prayerful. Lord, we know this isn't easy. Just help us to be obedient. Amen.

I rejoiced greatly in the Lord that at last you renewed your concern for me. Indeed, you were concerned, but you had no opportunity to show it. I am not saying this because I am in need, for I have learned to be content whatever the circumstances. I know what it is to be in need, and I know what it is to have plenty. I have learned the secret of being content in any and every situation, whether well fed or hungry, whether living in plenty or in want. Philippians 4:10–12

BEING CONTENT

My wife grew up in an Ohio home of modest means. She drove an old Volkswagen bug back and forth to college her junior and senior year. Her dad worked in the Ford factory for many years before this to get her through college. After finishing her bachelor's degree in teacher education, she obtained a masters and doctoral degree. She was married at the age of 28 and then had two children during her thirties. She worked to raise her children and support her family. As the children grew a bit older, she returned to work as a college professor. She experienced a lot of professional success and became chair of the faculty, the highest-respected community member amongst the faculty. Through all of this, she was a content person that valued her family relationships over professional success.

Then, the roof caved in. In her mid-50's, she started having trouble walking and controlling her fine dexterity skills. She had numb fingers. She lost muscular control of her limbs. She was out hunting one day and tripped over her feet and fell down on the side of a mountain. During the fall, she stuck her gun smack into the dirt. We helped her up and asked what was wrong. She said, "I don't know, but my balance is terrible." Shortly after this, she went to a neurologist who immediately diagnosed her with Multiple Sclerosis. Transitioning from the pinnacle of a professional career to the overwhelming news of having a serious chronic disease: How does one choose contentment when receiving this type of news?

Paul wrote the Philippians that he "rejoiced greatly" for their renewed care and concern for him as a person. Then in the same breath he talks about the importance of contentment. Paul urges his readers to be content regardless of the circumstances. Paul writes that he knows what it is to have plenty and what it means to be in need. Paul then points to the secret of being content whatever the circumstances. His secret is found in verse 13: "I can do all this through him who gives me strength." Paul depended upon Christ's resources.

A few years after being diagnosed with Multiple Sclerosis, my wife was on her way to a college class that was designed to discuss human movement and foundations of physical wellness, when, just as she walked through the doorway, she crashed to the floor, flat on her face in front of her class of students. You can imagine the shock on their faces. Shortly after this, it was clear that she was not going to be able to continue teaching, which clearly was one of her sources of contentment. She resigned shortly after this happened because of the risks involved for her and for her students.

Today, a couple of years later, she is content regardless of her circumstances. She is working within our local church as a Sunday school teacher. She is involved in the community with the Moms in Prayer organization. She is also teaching handicapped students in one-on-one Bible study. Thankfully, her contentment is a choice to rejoice in and celebrate each day that she can continue teaching others.

Prayer: Lord, thank you for allowing us to be content, regardless of our circumstances. We humbly appreciate that our source of contentment is our dependence on you whatever our circumstances. Guide us in the days ahead to be confident in the fact that whatever we do is for your glory. Amen.

Whoever spares the rod hates their children, but the one who loves their children is careful to discipline them. Proverbs 13:24

Discipline with Care

After the twins were born, we had a major dilemma in our home: who was going to be the disciplinarian in our home when dad was away? With two one-year-old children and one each at the ages of 4, 7, 9, 10, and 11, the "disciplining of the children" could have been a nightmare. From her hospital bed in the living room and her wheelchair, mom took the lead. She couldn't move her limbs. How did she discipline each of the children?

As one sibling said, "she disciplined us by either biting our finger or by biting our ear." You may ask yourself, what fool would stick their finger or ear in someone's mouth to be bitten? The dilemma was simple. Either have mom bite your finger or ear, or receive the "wrath" of the paddle discipline upon dad returning home from a day's work or a business trip.

Mom doled out her discipline carefully because otherwise it would have lost its effect. Usually the sequence went like this: First came a verbal correction and re-direction. This usually involved withholding an extrinsic reward, such as the other six children receiving cookies and the one child having them withheld until the behavior changed.

The next step of the discipline process usually included a carefully worded challenge framed by the potential denial of some intrinsic reward. My mother might say, "I'm growing tired of your behavior" or "I only have so much patience and is it fair that you are draining my energy with your misbehaviors?" Frankly, because mom was so careful with her discipline, we never wanted to disappoint her and it just crushed us to experience her disapproval. The depth of her love was evident each day in how she invested in each of the children. Somehow, she actually had eyes all over the house without moving around. She knew exactly which foods were in the pantry and she also knew intuitively when one of her children was misbehaving. Her discipline was seldom for an act of misconduct. Usually, the discipline occurred because of some type of inappropriate attitude. Our mom's careful discipline was associated with monitoring our attitudes.

Her last resort in the discipline process was a finger or ear bite. Whenever humility was lacking, or attitudes clashed, the child was instructed to step right next to the wheelchair or the hospital bed. Then she said, "Place your finger in my mouth." That was the "misdemeanor" discipline process. If a "felony" occurred (usually that just meant multiple misdemeanor offenses as defined by mom), we were told, "Place your ear in my mouth."

The immediate response was usually a shriek of screaming with pain and instantaneous tears. Whether it hurt that much or not, we learned to demonstrate remorse fairly quickly. After the physical pain was inflicted, then came the closing careful part of the discipline. Without hesitating, mom's next words were, "Remember, I love you." Perhaps strange from your perspective, but this discipline process formidably shaped each of the children into who we are today.

Prayer: Lord, thank you for the careful discipline we can provide and receive from others. May we be careful within a context of love. Instead of yelling, help us Lord to guide our constructive discipline with your biblical principles of love, grace, and truth. Amen.

> Rather, as servants of God we commend ourselves in every way: in great endurance; in troubles, hardships and distresses; . . . sorrowful, yet always rejoicing; poor, yet making many rich; having nothing, and yet possessing everything. 2 Corinthians 6:4 & 10

TRUE COMMENDATION

Most look for commendation through trying to be recognized. Human nature in its fallen state strives for recognition by friends, working colleagues, and sometimes even family. However, commending ourselves to another is a matter of setting priorities regardless of circumstances. Accolades are fleeting but the innate desire to bring recognition to oneself is human nature. This Scripture verse calls us to a different kind of recognition. Seeking to serve God to bring glory to his name in "every" way is true commendation. "Every" is the key word here because we are called to give 100 percent of our lives regardless of the circumstances.

At the age of 33, my wife had our first child. During almost 24 hours of childbirth, the painstaking results were nearly fatal. After delivering the baby, my wife had a situation where internal bleeding caused her blood pressure to drop dramatically. The doctor was finished with his responsibilities. The nurse promptly gave me our newborn and screamed "get out" of the room. I held our baby daughter and listened to the drama. The nurse pressed the code blue button and yelled into the monitor, no pulse and her blood pressure has bottomed out. To save my wife, the on-call physician quickly adjusted the bed to raise her pelvis higher than her head in the Trendelenburg position. After being tipped on her head with feet well above the head, blood returned to her heart and her blood pressure slowly returned to 40/20, 50/30, 60/40, and 90/60.

After this experience, my spouse began to give everything away; something I can only commend her for doing so graciously. The first thing she gave away was her career. Although she was a Ph.D. trained college educator, she decided straightaway to forego teaching and administrative duties for thirteen years. She was humbly willing to give 100 percent of herself away to invest in our covenant children. Please don't mistake the claim here. There are many working mothers who give themselves away to their families and do a great job while working in a called profession. But, after the experience with the traumatic childbirth, my wife just decided it was an opportunity to invest in her children in every way. After the children were both in grade school, she transitioned back to work as a college professor and a department chair.

Fast forward to age 53. The children are grown up and out of the home or off to college. My wife's diagnosis this time around was the devastating news of Multiple Sclerosis. In a few short years, she found herself in trouble, hardship, and distress again. She went from being able to run, bike, and play tennis to being unable to even walk without stabilizing assistance. It was devastating having to quit doing the profession she loved – teaching college students. Remember the Scripture verse above that references being "sorrowful, yet always rejoicing; poor, yet making many rich; having nothing yet possessing everything." She went from having everything to having nothing when it came to the joy of human movement.

True commendation involves serving God in every way. Now, instead of teaching college students, my wife finds herself in a prayer ministry for others. There will be many times when she stops me and re-directs me to pray for a family instead of coming to a conclusion that is assuming or short-sighted. She now teaches a Sunday school class (while sitting down) and is giving herself away again in every way. She has nothing, but possesses everything because she is seeking true commendation.

Prayer: Lord, help us to seek accolades that allow us to give ourselves away rather than seeking commendation for the wrong reasons. Guide our habits of seeking recognition and allow us in all aspects of our lives to worship you. May this worship be a liturgy that is God-honoring to you and you alone. Amen.

CALLED TO SACRIFICE ON A DAILY BASIS

My wife and I waited to get married because of professional
aspirations to finish academic degrees. My wife was 28. I was 24.
Three years into our marriage we knew that some (more) important decisions were in the offing. The discussions were really, really
serious because she was facing the delivery of our first child Lindsay. The decision on the table was related to whether she would stay
at home and focus predominantly on raising the children. My wife
had just finished her Ph.D. and defended her dissertation while being eight months pregnant. Think about this sacrifice. Professional
development was a top priority for her because both her parents
only had a high school education. She had just finished an achievement that took 31 years to fully accomplish.

Having just finished her doctorate, now the decision at hand
was to stay home or continue to work. After the delivery and the
ensuing trauma of our daughter Lindsay's birth, she decided to stay
at home to be with the children. A few short months later, she offered a different sacrifice. The vice president for academic affairs at
our college was on Continental flight 1713 when it crashed on the
Denver International Airport runway. As one of the few survivors,
he suffered serious brain trauma and was unable to return to work.
Because of her teacher education training, my spouse was asked
to return to work in the teacher education department to fill the
spot of a professor who was being promoted to be the interim vice
president for academic affairs.

This snapshot of life was just a sample illustration of how my
spouse sacrificed on a daily basis to help others. While she was glad
to return to professional work, it really was only made possible by
a friend that came and babysat our infant daughter during the full
year. True sacrifices are usually only possible when others chip in
and help make it happen. This family friend essentially "gave away"
a year of her life to allow my wife to help an institution that was in
a dire situation due to a terrible airplane accident.

When I reflect on my spouse's and this friend's sacrifice to care for our newborn, I challenge myself to consider how we should consider offering daily sacrifices as fragrant love offerings. Christ's body and blood sacrificial love offering is the ultimate example for all of us. The sacrifices we make pale in comparison to Christ's ultimate gift but we should nonetheless think intentionally about how we can help others.

After my wife completed her year back in the classroom, my wife's brother and sister-in-law moved to the area where we were living. They too had a newborn. My wife then took the next year to care for this infant nephew, just as our good friend had taken care of our daughter the previous year. What better way to sacrifice than to remember how you have been helped and in turn give yourself away in a similar manner.

Prayer: Lord, thank you for the sacrifice friends and family demonstrate in our daily lives. Thank you also for providing us opportunities to sacrifice our time, talents, and resources to share with others. We humbly understand that this doesn't match your ultimate sacrifice, but we are grateful that you call us to give ourselves away on a daily basis. May these acts be a fragrant offering to you. Amen.

Jesus said to them, "Surely you will quote this proverb to me: 'Physician, heal yourself.' And you will tell me, 'Do here in your hometown what we have heard that you did in Capernaum.'" "Truly I tell you," he continued, "no prophet is accepted in his hometown." Luke 4:23–24

HEAL YOURSELF

In the journey with Multiple Sclerosis, there are people who try to link past sin with a person's current health status. As we read this Scripture on healing, even a physician from his hometown is challenged to do what only God can perform. Do you ever find yourself wishing to be cured from a mild infirmity or recent malady? Or perhaps you have a desire to be healed from something even more serious? I can attest that physical healing is only part of what we need on this earth. We need healing from much more than this. We need to seek God to help us first in the healing of our liturgies (and inappropriate idols) and habits. The Scripture verse suggests that no prophet is accepted in his hometown. Why is this? Because most people who share prophetic thoughts in their hometown are dismissed as being aloof, arrogant, or irreverent. The problem with sharing prophecy in your hometown is that people most often don't want to hear about cleaning up their habits. Perhaps you are struggling with a not so obvious habit of anger, poor attitude, or simply ungratefulness. Perhaps you are struggling with a physical addiction related to alcohol, smoking, a prescription, or misuse of over-the-counter medications. Regardless what it is, perhaps God is asking in this verse, "Do you really need my help?" Should you listen to a friend in your hometown that is trying to encourage you to simply overcome a sin that is hard to shake?

The exciting challenge here is to consider focusing on the root of these kinds of habits rather than asking God for some kind of miraculous healing of one's limitations. Physical limitations are usually temporary. Habits start in the heart and mind. Scripture continually guides us to focus less on the physical and more on transformational thoughts and actions. Is there a reason why we as humans focus too much on the physical? Yes, because we want to be healed by the Great Physician. The truth is that the Great Physician is ready to heal us. Healing at the root starts with heart, head, and hand healing. Heart healing is for us to first check our motives. Are they pure? Head healing is checking our habits and asking ourselves whether we have the responsibility to move into purer habits – versus asking God to heal us of our obvious or self-inflicted infirmities. Hand healing means we move towards helping our brother and sister and focus less on ourselves. All three of these opportunities also help bring us true healing.

Prayer: Lord, help us not to focus on infirmities that are passing maladies that involve requests for quick physician "fixes" when in reality we bring habits to the table that can be overcome with thoughtful, heartfelt actions of changed attitudes and actions. Forgive us Lord for a focus on ourselves versus focusing on others. Transform our liturgies (habits) Lord to honor you in your Kingdom. Thank you for healing us. Amen.

JESUS, LORD OF ALL

I asked one of my siblings, "What in your estimation was mom's contribution to her community and to the world?" The sibling responded, "Joy in the midst of suffering was vividly impressed upon our minds. All of this was her testimony to the lordship and goodness of Jesus Christ."

Each day, our mother put on a new self. She often renewed herself in three different ways. One, she renewed herself by consuming God's word on a daily basis. Second, she renewed herself daily by living a joy-filled life. Third, in embracing the creational design of all individuals as being created in the image of God she acknowledged the lordship of Jesus Christ.

Her consuming of God's Word on a daily basis was made possible by a generous organization that helped individuals that were deaf and/or blind. This special organization recorded all the books of the Bible on tape. Shortly after this taping technology was completed, the organization offered the tapes to other individuals as well. Every day mom would listen to chapter after chapter of the Bible. During the week, this often involved listening to whole books. We would press the play button on the tape player when leaving for school and she would listen to the entire tape before it turned itself off. She lived in God's Word and she lived out God's Word. She renewed herself in the knowledge and the image of her Creator.

A second practice mom displayed was living a joy-filled life. Each morning, with an unbelievably positive disposition, she would be vaulted out of bed. Then she was taken to the bathroom. After this, she was placed in her wheelchair and wheeled out to the hospital bed in the living room. She was then placed on the hospital bed for the remainder of the day before she would go to bed 14 hours later. Each morning for over 24 years, she was positive and joy-filled, although she had every reason in the world to be a grump in the morning. She couldn't walk. All she did each day was to look out the picture window into God's creation of the Colorado outdoors. Somewhere deep inside of her, she had the knowledge of her Creator and she displayed his image every day. Regardless of circumstances, her face glowed with his image on a daily basis. It seems nearly impossible, but those who knew her daily disposition will vouch for this truth.

Lastly, mom was a bucket-filler. She saw the promise of God in all individuals. Because she acknowledged God as Creator, she was able to encourage single moms on their journey. She valued a redemptive and restorative approach. Many of the unwed mothers who helped take care of mom and the family was a different person when they left than when they first arrived. Many of the unwed mothers arrived downtrodden and broken. Through a day-to-day exposure to a redemptive and restorative approach, mom was able to be a powerful witness. Sure, these mothers made a mistake and they fell short. But, we all have fallen short and we are responsible for putting on a new self. Perhaps simply said, mom had a way of seeing in a mirror clearly how to live out Christ-like values and encourage others in becoming better image-bearers of our Creator. She did this primarily by demonstrating joy in the midst of suffering.

Prayer: Thank you Lord for giving us an opportunity to demonstrate joy in all aspects of our life. Help us live in gratitude because of your lordship and goodness. Forgive us when we fall short in our thoughts, actions, attitudes, and dispositions. Help us to look outside ourselves and put on a new self each day. Shape us in your image. Amen.

> Do not be anxious about anything, but in every situation, by prayer and petition, with thanksgiving, present your requests to God. Philippians 4:6

OVERCOMING ANXIETY BY LEADING WITH GRATITUDE

Picture the thoughts running through my mind as a six-year-old. My mother was just diagnosed with Multiple Sclerosis and we just had twin infants. Desperation, anxiety, denial, anger, surprise, concern, and being overwhelmed were some of my emotions during the first years of the diagnosis. Imagine a six-year-old thinking about six other brothers and sisters under the age of ten having a mother that couldn't walk or take care of the infant babies. It was an unbelievable time of anxiety and worry about the future. Some of the immediate thoughts that came to mind included projecting dismal circumstances near into the future. Some of these thoughts included feelings of a short life expectancy for mom and all the other gamut of emotions that can be processed by a six-year-old. My six-year-old mind truly wondered whether my mom would die and about who would take care of us.

My relationship with my mother was one of transparency. She allowed the young children to ask any question they wanted. I initially would ask about the "why" of the disease and how we can deal with this as a family? The first words out of my mother's mouth were consistently, "Everything is going to be okay." Shortly after mentioning that everything would be okay, she would lead with words of gratitude. She would share about the importance of having a healthy mind. She expressed her commitment to her children and indicated that her only prayer was that before she passed and let go of her frail earthly body that she would be able to guide all her children through high school.

Mom was the most prayerful woman I've ever met. She wasn't a person that prayed charismatically. She was a person that prayed "in the closet" and very few people knew about it. She was a person that prayed when it was quiet and she was alone on her hospital bed. Her ability to listen to someone's petition, share positive words of gratitude and encouragement, and then pray for her children or her friends was a daily commitment in her life. She wasn't a saint. But her life of devotion to interceding on behalf of others was fairly close to this higher order.

Fast forward a few years later, when common childhood anxieties were ever present. Our parents helped us overcome these anxieties by encouraging gratitude for the simple aspects of life. Examples of this included encouraging us to be thankful for the blessing of food. We didn't have very much, but somehow the loaves and fishes were enough for the evening meal, even though seconds weren't available. We were encouraged to be grateful for clothes. Most of us had only two or three different outfits in the early years. Because I was the first boy, without hand-me-downs from older siblings, the pickings were extremely slim. Not having worldly goods just didn't matter though, because when we were taught to live in gratitude and live simply, the anxiety was minimized.

Through trials, some of which included various forms of anxiety, we learned a valuable lesson: start with an attitude of thankfulness. It wasn't a utopian perspective. It was a kingdom focus perspective modeled by our mom exuding patience and kindness through her physical trials. This impressionable practice was, without a doubt, one of the largest legacies of our mother's influence.

Prayer: Lord, we have so many reasons to be anxious. Forgive us Lord when we allow anxieties to rule our lives. Help us to pray in a spirit of gratitude. Allow us to remember to be grateful for all you do for us. Thank you for our daily bread. Thank you for family. Thank you for trials. Thank you for answered prayer and for allowing us to approach you with petitions. Amen.

To some who were confident of their own righteousness and looked down on everyone else, Jesus told this parable: "Two men went up to the temple to pray, one a Pharisee and the other a tax collector. The Pharisee stood by himself and prayed: 'God, I thank you that I am not like other people – robbers, evildoers, adulterers – or even like this tax collector. I fast twice a week and give a tenth of all I get.' But the tax collector stood at a distance. He would not even look up to heaven, but beat his breast and said, 'God, have mercy on me, a sinner.' I tell you that this man, rather than the other, went home justified before God. For all those who exalt themselves will be humbled, and those who humble themselves will be exalted." Luke 18:9–14

TRUE HUMILITY

True humility is hard to find these days, but sometimes our circumstances cause us to reflect on our level of humility. This was definitely true for our mother, and we, her children, noticed. Specific experiences that caught our attention with mom's declining health and ensuing healthcare needs include:

- A rapid initial decline of mom's health led to falling in public places, causing emotional scars and accompanying tears.
- After the M.S. diagnosis, using a cane made walking easier.
- A few months later, a walker provided better stability for walking.
- Shortly after trying other available technologies, a wheel chair was the last resort.
- Loss of muscular control and muscle spasms marked the next step.
- Then came bladder complications and the loss of voluntary urinary control.
- Vocal chords were affected next and we could only understand her words by reading her lips.
- When we were out in public with seven children and two parents, we consistently had unwed mothers with us, which turned plenty of heads and prompted unique conversations.

The list could go on. Hopefully these word pictures are enough to illustrate that mom's experiences made her more of a tax collector than a Pharisee. She would often be caught in unfortunate circumstances that could have caused unbelievable and understandable frustration. She could have become angry about not being able to walk. She could have displaced her emotions onto someone close by when her muscle spasms were uncontrollable (at the time, her medications were not that effective in controlling spasticity). She could have become bitter when someone other than her spouse had to take her to the bathroom.

Probably the toughest of situations included the loss of her ability to articulate words in a clear manner. All seven children learned to read lips. During this challenging time of transition to lip reading, mom could have become unbelievably frustrated. There were plenty of tensions as we tried to understand her. It was very trying for her to repeat comments time after time. Somehow, mom was a picture of patience through these emotional times.

How was it possible to demonstrate so much patience in dealing with the progressive crippling of Multiple Sclerosis? It was only possible by the practice of humility. She somehow lived in gratitude despite her circumstances. Her practice of thinking of others first was the way she lived out her humility. She was not interested in exalting herself. She found a way to exalt others by giving them undivided attention and sincerely praying for them. All of this was only possible by crying out for mercy and humbly asking for God's help in less than fortunate circumstances.

Prayer: Thank you for the lessons in humility that we were able to learn from a mother that modeled unbelievable patience. Help us Lord to stay humble and to think of others before ourselves. Amen.

He says, "Be still, and know that I am God; I will be exalted among the nations, I will be exalted in the earth." Psalm 46:10

BEING ABLE TO CEASE STRIVING

Be still and know that I am God. This is a courageous goal that involves slowing down and being willing to cease striving. Before my mother was diagnosed with Multiple Sclerosis, she was a type A, highly driven individual. She was active in her church. She was musically talented and even cut a recording of high profile music. She would plan her day out with seven children, who at one time were all under the age of ten. A frenetic hustle and bustle was the order of the day.

Fast forward thirty years to my spouse's diagnosis with Multiple Sclerosis. During her high school years, she was a talented student-athlete. At college she competed as a four sport athlete in volleyball, basketball, track, and tennis. In all of her years of college tennis, she never lost a match. For these accolades, she was recently inducted into her college's athletic hall of fame. Picture a driven person like this suddenly stricken with a very aggressive form of M.S. and having to slow down her pace of life.

As a type "A" person, my spouse learned to be still after the diagnosis. I'm guilty of also being too driven, so I've been privileged to observe my wife:

- stopping more frequently during the day to pray and meditate;
- expanding her reading of Scripture and books that have helped her grow in a theological perspective;
- enjoying the routine aspects of daily living and celebrating simple physical accomplishments;
- losing perspective less frequently and having unbelievable patience in trying circumstances.

And when human beings acknowledge the importance of being still, God's glory is placed in proper perspective. As the Scripture verse says, "I will be exalted among the nations, I will be exalted in the earth."

What are some real life illustrations of this within the trauma of experiencing M.S.? The other day, I wanted my wife to agree with my opinion about a serious situation in the community. Instead of supporting my opinion, she paused and encouraged me to pray for the individual and the situation. Rather than reinforcing my opinion, which really wasn't going to solve anything of substance, her being still with a prayerful approach worked much, much better. God was exalted, and it was amazing to see how doing so resolved a deep-seated issue.

Time and again, I have been humbled by how my spouse has modeled being still. Instead of manipulating a situation, she approaches life more slowly and uses Scripture to inform all she does. Instead of expecting an expedient resolution with an "easy answer," she now takes a longer approach to problem-solving. There is much to learn from this approach of being still.

What the NIV renders as "be still" the New American Standard Bible translates as "cease striving." There are so many areas in our lives where we could benefit from ceasing to strive. We live in a world that rewards goal achievement and reaching objectives. Instead, we are called to slow down and ask God to guide situations with his providential hand. Instead of seeking easy answers to complex conundrums, we should seek solutions by allowing time, stillness, and prayer to improve the quality of our decisions.

Prayer: Lord, help me make a conscious effort to slow down and be still. Help us all to be intentional about giving you the glory and exalting you as our God. Only then can the end result of our decisions and circumstances be a blessing beyond comprehension. Thank you for allowing us to cease striving. Amen.

Therefore [Jesus] is able to save completely those who come to God through him, because he always lives to intercede for them. Such a high priest truly meets our need – one who is holy, blameless, pure, set apart from sinners, exalted above the heavens. Unlike the other high priests, he does not need to offer sacrifices day after day, first for his own sins, and then for the sins of the people. He sacrificed for their sins once for all when he offered himself. Hebrews 7:25–27

CALLED TO LIVE DIFFERENTLY

Christ was the atoning sacrifice for our sins and he has the power to intercede for us before the throne of the Almighty. Instead of the priests regularly offering animal sacrifices on the altar, first for themselves and then for the people, Christ offered himself once and for all as the ultimate sacrifice for our sins.

In his actions and attitudes, Christ modeled the ultimate sacrifice of giving himself away. By living a holy, blameless, pure, and sinless life Christ modeled a way to live differently. Through my mother's modeling, we also learned to live differently. Through her positive actions while overcoming day-to-day challenges, she illustrated how to live in a sanctified and holy manner. She would challenge each of her children to be more graceful in their daily habits and interactions. She attempted to be blameless by interceding and offering support when we had fallen short of our calling as children of God.

Our shortcomings as children could have caused our parents great disappointment. A few illustrations of falling short include the following:
- One of the seven children experienced a pregnancy before marriage.
- Another sibling's marriage ended in divorce.
- One sibling started smoking cigarettes at a relatively young age.
- One other sibling was involved in substance abuse.

(Incidentally, our parents consistently warned us against the abuse of alcohol. There was a clear genetic reason for this. Three of my father's four siblings ended up as alcoholics.) Even though these things happened within our family, my mother didn't throw away the gift of grace. When she would learn of an unexpected misstep by one of her children, she did her best to live blamelessly. She demonstrated patience, walking with them through the valleys and the peaks, and offering wisdom and guidance to overcome various challenging circumstances.

Most of all, mom put her pride aside. I'm sure she was tempted to be angry and grieved, and inclined to distance herself from us. Instead of these worldly responses, mom was somehow able to be set apart – holy – in her responses. Mom interceded with patience, prayer, and ample supplies of biblical wisdom. This ability to humbly respond helped us see that mom was willing to worry less about her pride and more about how to give God the glory. These responses helped each of us through a variety of challenging human circumstances.

Prayer: Lord, help us to be set apart in our actions and attitudes. Realistically, you are the only one who lived blamelessly. Forgive us when we fall short, but inspire us to strive more to extend grace and truth in all circumstances. Humbly allow us to learn your pure ways of holy living. Amen.

Praise be to the God and Father of our Lord Jesus Christ! In his great mercy he has given us new birth into a living hope through the resurrection of Jesus Christ from the dead, and into an inheritance that can never perish, spoil or fade. This inheritance is kept in heaven for you, who through faith are shielded by God's power until the coming of the salvation that is ready to be revealed in the last time. In all this you greatly rejoice, though now for a little while you may have had to suffer grief in all kinds of trials. These have come so that the proven genuineness of your faith – of greater worth than gold, which perishes even though refined by fire – may result in praise, glory and honor when Jesus Christ is revealed. 1 Peter 1:3–7

CALLED TO REJOICE

One of the great paradoxes of the Christian life is found in these verses. Not surprisingly, these verses in 1ˢᵗ Peter call us to praise God in all circumstances of life, whether we are in times of grief or times of plenty. One of my siblings asked my father to list some words that came to mind when thinking about the challenges of dealing with a spouse inflicted by Multiple Sclerosis. Some of these included: early symptoms, close calls, burn-out, car accidents, and increased intelligence.

Peter's mention of having had to "suffer grief" calls us to consider how we can still rejoice by exemplifying "greater worth than gold" by living faithfully in obedience to God's will. These verses are a litany of calls to rejoice. First comes: "Praise be to the God and Father of our Lord Jesus Christ!" Then we are asked to contemplate our living hope. The theme of inheritance is introduced and a promise that never perishes including being shielded by God's power. Because of the promise of salvation that will be ready to be revealed in the last time, we are called to greatly rejoice!

Then the qualifier of the verse calls us to recognize that while we may have had to suffer grief in all kinds of trials, this will be an opportunity to prove the genuineness of our faith. All of this "may" result in praise, glory and honor when Jesus Christ is revealed. The word "may" strikingly sticks out here because it is a qualifier for those who have suffered grief in all their trials and have kept a spirit of rejoicing. Yes, we are called to rejoice all the time. The meaning of this rejoicing is found in the promise of salvation.

Put yourself in my dad's shoes as he watched his spouse falling for unknown reasons in the yard, losing her ability to speak clearly, and gradually becoming unable to care for the many physical needs of seven children under the age of ten. Eventually, his wife took five minutes to walk from the car to the store. She had a car accident because of being unable to have a normal response time with muscular control. Then reflect upon close calls of blood clots in the lungs, life-threatening pneumonia, excruciating bladder infections, and muscle spasms that were uncontrollable.

Through all these trials, the body can somehow take on an increased intelligence, including a photographic memory capacity. Somehow my mom responded to these trials with praise, rejoicing, and a daily demonstrated faith. It is only possible by the promise that we are refined by fire in preparation for Christ being revealed in a new heaven and earth.

Prayer: Lord, give us a spirit of praise and rejoicing despite our circumstances. Help us to acknowledge you as our living hope and in preparation for the final revelation of your salvation. Between this time of our present trials and a new heaven and new earth, give us a spirit of great rejoicing and also give us family and friends that demonstrate this genuine faith. We stand on your promises Lord of this being a temporary time of a refining fire that will lead into your salvation. Amen.

There is a time for everything, and a season for every activity under the heavens: a time to be born and a time to die, a time to plant and a time to uproot, a time to kill and a time to heal, a time to tear down and a time to build, a time to weep and a time to laugh, a time to mourn and a time to dance. . . . Ecclesiastes 3:1–4

HAVING A SENSE OF HUMOR AND BALANCE

A sense of humor is so valuable in life. We were so fortunate to see a keen sense of humor in our mom's life. This showed up at impromptu times, such as during meals. Every morning before breakfast, we had to give mom a stack of pills. This was early in the morning before school started, and it was miserable and tedious for the young children because it took forever. Mom would start into a laughing spell all because those darn pills were next to impossible to swallow with the closing of her trachea. We finally found a way to conquer the giggles and the sad moments that M.S. causes. One day, by trial and error, we discovered yogurt was a masterful lubricant for all those crazy pills. Finally, we found an efficient way to feed the pills without the water, straw, and swallow method.

Through all this feeding and taking of pills, we learned lessons about life. As the Scripture above says, there is an appropriate season to weep and an appropriate season to laugh. Without a doubt, our family found both of these seasons to be plentiful. How about you? Are you able to keep a balance and make sure that humor is an integral part of your life?

The answer to keeping a balance is the perspective found in Ecclesiastes. There is a season for every activity. The Bible calls us to celebrate (laugh) when a newborn child is brought into this world or an adoption occurs. When new beginnings occur, we are to rejoice with those who rejoice. There is also an appropriate time to pause and pay respects when life on earth comes to an end. During this time, humor is most often out of place.

These sequential verses emphasize that there is also an appropriate time to plant (start something new) and find humor and joy in this new beginning. There is a time to have the crops harvested and uproot and move onto new adventures. In honoring beginnings and endings, we are to keep a balance. Keeping a balance also acknowledges there is a time to harvest and a time designated for healing. Isn't it ironic that even in observing seasons for farming, fall and early winter involves harvesting? Winter and early spring bring about "healing" and time for rest. Late spring and summer are designated for planting and growth. A season is defined by a period of time that God designed intentionally well.

The verses continue on with guidance on tearing down and building up. This can have symbolic farming implications, but there is something deeper. There is a human touch that should be emphasized. Whenever we offer someone a constructive critique, the Scripture instructs us to encourage and build one another up as well. It is interesting to note that the (negative) tear down precedes the (positive) build up; but in half of the references the positive comes first. There is a lesson there too.

Weeping, laughing, mourning, and dancing conclude this portion of verses. These are just yardsticks of instruction for us to maintain a balance. We are essentially called to be respectful of God's timing. Let's return to the pill illustration. A sense of humor was invaluable until we found the natural potion of yogurt. The underlying lesson here is to enjoy the seasons, keep a balance, and trust God's timing.

Prayer: Lord, help us to seek a balance. Forgive us when we are impatient with seasons of life. Amen.

INDEX OF SCRIPTURE REFERENCES

Eric Forseth (Ph.D., The Ohio State University) lives out his passion for education and serving others through his role as the Dordt College provost. Eric and his wife, Kim, have served in Christian education for almost 35 years. An avid outdoorsman, Eric enjoys spending free time hunting, fishing, golfing, and riding his road bike. They have two children, Lindsay Grant and Nathan Forseth. Lindsay is the mother of two children, Jenaye and Natalie, is a college professor, and resides In Idaho with her husband Tyler. Nathan lives in Boston, MA and works for a division of Rolls-Royce that serves the U.S. Navy.

Multiple Sclerosis (MS) is an auto-immune disease that first manifests itself by hindering the individual's motor capabilities. The individual's white blood cells mistake the body's nerve cells for contagions that need to be destroyed. White blood cells eat away at the myelin sheath that allow electrical signals to pass from one nerve ending to another. The decreased electrical conductivity of nerves in the brain and spine can lead to tremors, decreased motor capabilities, and paralysis in extreme cases. MS is not known to be genetic, and there is currently no known cure.

CPSIA information can be obtained
at www.ICGtesting.com
Printed in the USA
FFOW04n1639131016
28463FF